SEASH

ANDREW CLEAVE

HAMLYN

HOW TO USE THIS BOOK

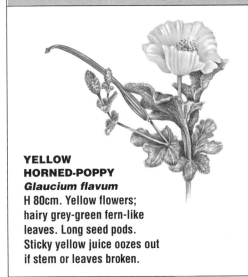

**YELLOW
HORNED-POPPY**
Glaucium flavum
H 80cm. Yellow flowers;
hairy grey-green fern-like
leaves. Long seed pods.
Sticky yellow juice oozes out
if stem or leaves broken.

This guide covers over 200 seashore
species likely to be found around the UK.
The entries on the identification pages
(46-125) give, where applicable, the
common English name (or names), and
scientific name in italics. (Each species,
whether plant, insect or animal, has a
scientific name of two words which is
unique to it. With seashore species, the
scientific name is important because
many species do not have distinguishing
common English names.) Significant
dimensions - height (H), length (L),
diameter (D) and width (W) - are given
in metric measurements, followed by
some useful information, on
identification or habits, for example.

ACKNOWLEDGEMENTS

The author and publishers would like to thank the
following individuals for their assistance in the
preparation of this book: Andrew Branson of British
Wildlife Publishing, Principal Consultant · David
Christie, Editorial Consultant · and Derek Hall,
who conceived the series.

Published in 1991 by
Hamlyn Children's Books,
part of Reed International Books,
Michelin House, 81 Fulham Road,
London SW3 6RB

ISBN 0 600 56949 7

Printed in Portugal

CONTENTS

SEASHORES

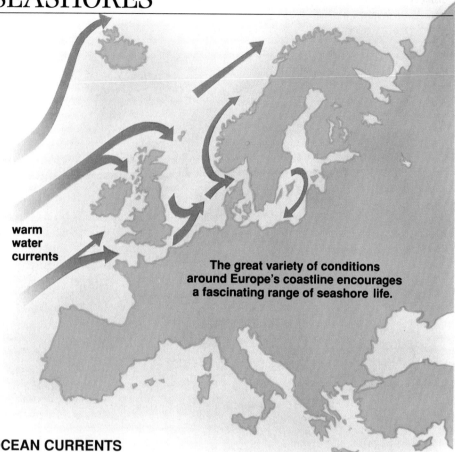

warm water currents

The great variety of conditions around Europe's coastline encourages a fascinating range of seashore life.

OCEAN CURRENTS

The wildlife that can be found on a seashore depends on the effects of ocean currents, tides, the variation in shelter, and temperature. In tropical regions the heat of the sun warms the ocean. This causes currents of warmer water to flow towards colder regions. When the currents hit islands or continents they change direction. In the North Atlantic, warm water from the tropics flows north and cold water from beneath the polar ice cap flows south to replace it. Thus, warm water from the Gulf of Mexico flows towards western Europe and gives it a mild climate. This current is called the Gulf Stream, or North Atlantic Drift.

The warm Gulf Stream cools as it reaches Iceland and Scandinavia and cold water from the polar ice cap replaces it. The ocean currents carry nutrients and organisms vast distances.

Tides ▷

As the Earth revolves around the Sun, the waters of the oceans and seas move with it, and the Sun exerts a pull on the water. The Moon, too, exerts a pull on the water, as it revolves around the Earth. When the Sun and Moon are in line, during the times of a new Moon or full Moon, they exert the greatest pull on the oceans and the highest tides result. When the Moon and Sun are pulling against each other, during the time of half Moon, the lowest tides result. Gradually the tides change from the highest, or spring tides, to the lowest, or neap tides.

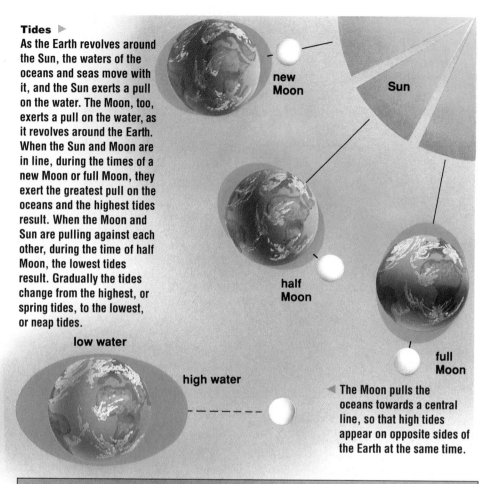

new Moon

Sun

half Moon

full Moon

low water

high water

◁ The Moon pulls the oceans towards a central line, so that high tides appear on opposite sides of the Earth at the same time.

TIDES AND TIMETABLES

Twice a day the tide rises and falls. As full Moon approaches, so the tide reaches further up the shore, and retreats further. As the Moon wanes, the tides reach less far up the shore. Every day the high-water time is a few minutes later, and high tide reaches a different level on the shore. The time of each high tide is also different for each stretch of coastline, so tide timetables are published to give this information. Look in newspapers, or on harbours, for tide timetables. You can buy tide timetables at chandleries.

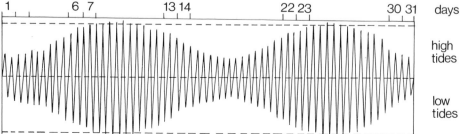

days: 1 6 7 13 14 22 23 30 31

high tides

low tides

CURRENTS AND TIDES

Wherever there is a river mouth, a projecting headland or a narrow stretch of water between an island and the mainland, there will be strong currents; when the tide is halfway out or halfway in the currents will be at their strongest, so great care should be taken by swimmers or sailors. These currents carry food in the form of microscopic plants and animals, which are in turn food for fish, birds and sea mammals. The currents also carry debris, which is deposited on the shore at high tide. At the highest spring tide everything is pushed far up the shore, but as each tide becomes lower, a new drift line forms further down the beach.

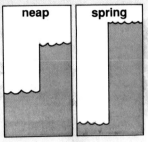

During neap tides the rise and fall is not great and the currents are weakest, but during spring tides the currents are stronger and the tides have a greater range.

lower shore

low spring tide

avera tide

Some organisms can ▶
travel for vast distances
across the oceans, even
though they are quite unable
to swim on their own.
Several species of tropical
trees produce floating seeds
which can cross the Atlantic
and reach Europe. They often
turn up after westerly gales,
such as these sea beans
found in Cornwall.

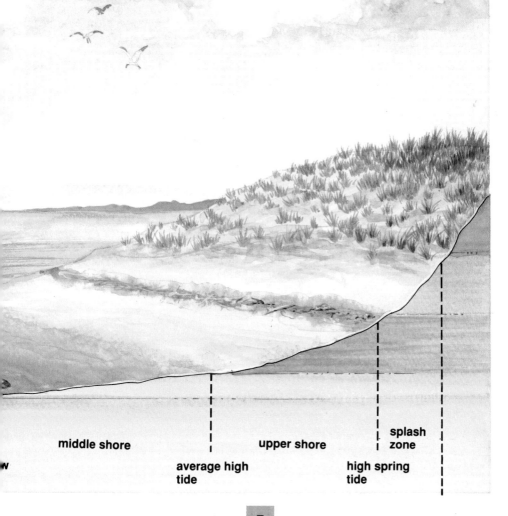

middle shore

average high
tide

upper shore

splash
zone

high spring
tide

FIELD EQUIPMENT

In order to find plants and animals on the seashore some simple equipment is needed. Glass should be avoided because of the risk of breakages, and metal objects are also best avoided because of the damage that seawater can do to them. Wherever possible use plastic or wooden materials. A long-handled net is useful for catching creatures which live in deep water or under overhangs. A plastic bucket or washing-up bowl can then be used to examine the contents of the net. A garden spade can be used on sandy or muddy shores to dig for buried molluscs or worms. It is a good idea to have a strong bag to carry everything.

A magnifying glass will be needed to identify very small creatures, and it helps when watching the way in which organisms move or feed. Tie a string around it so that it can hang around your neck.

When using binoculars, if possible sit on a rock or lean against one and support your arms. Practise focusing on an object such as a distant lighthouse. Try scanning slowly along the shoreline, then the distant horizon. Always move the binoculars slowly. Wipe your hands if they are wet, and always clean the spray from binoculars with a soft cloth at the end of the day.

The correct clothing and footwear are essential for working on the seashore. Use old plimsolls for paddling, and wear a hat in very sunny weather to avoid heatstroke. Shirts with collars and long sleeves will help to prevent sunburn, which can be very painful. In winter and in stormy weather warm waterproof clothing, preferably in bright colours, will be more comfortable.

PROJECT

A viewing pail can be used to look into deep pools and see more clearly what is at the bottom. It can be made out of an old plastic bucket. Carefully cut a hole in the bottom of a plastic bucket, leaving a lip of at least 20mm. Clear perspex must be fixed into the bottom of the bucket with a watertight seal; aquarium sealant can be used for this. If the viewing pail is gently pushed down into the water it will help you to see the bottom of the pool; you will need to look into it very closely to get the best result. A simple viewing pail can be made by fixing thin plastic film across the end of a bucket or a piece of plastic tubing, but it will not be very sturdy.

plastic film

rubber band

perspex

cut bottom from bucket

HOME STUDY

Some specimens from the seashore can be taken home for further study. Empty shells, pieces of driftwood, seaweeds thrown up on the strandline and samples of mud and sand are all worth further study. Living specimens should be taken away from the shore only if you know you will be able to look after them and return them safely as soon as possible. Many marine organisms are very small and can be seen only with the aid of a good hand lens or a microscope. Only very small samples are needed for study under a microscope. It will be very helpful for looking at some of the encrusting organisms which live on shells or seaweeds, because many of these can be identified properly only if they are highly magnified.

Specimens
Remember that all marine organisms must spend at least some of their time immersed in the sea, so don't take them home if you can't provide suitable conditions. Also, take only small quantities; never remove every single specimen of a creature you find as you may wipe out a whole colony of a rare species if they die.

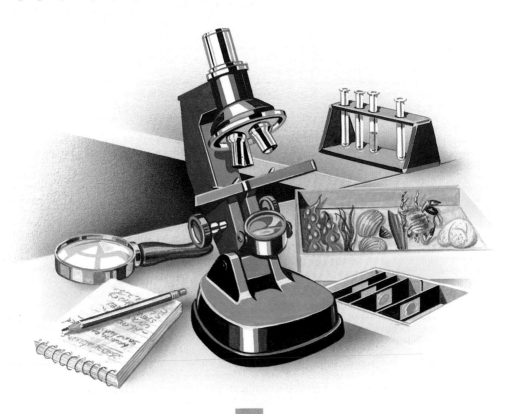

Seaweeds make very good pressed specimens. Float them on to a sheet of paper in a tray of water and arrange them to look lifelike. Drain off the water, cover the seaweed with muslin, and press the paper between sheets of newspaper under a heavy weight for a few days.

PROJECT

Why not make a marine aquarium? It must be made entirely of glass because metals corrode in salt water. Use a strong sealant to bind the glass sides to a thicker glass base. When it is dry, test it with tap water and rinse thoroughly. ▼

When the aquarium has been filled, it should be left to stand for a few days before any creatures are put in it. It will need an air pump to keep the water fresh and a filter to keep it clean. Do not put in the aquarium any creatures which will eat each other; return to the sea any which look unhappy.

Rocks and shells can be ▲ placed in it to give a natural effect and provide shelter for the inhabitants.

Stand the aquarium out of ▷ any direct sunlight. Place a thick layer of washed gravel and stones on the bottom, then fill it gently with fresh seawater.

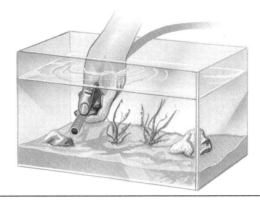

NETTING AND CATCHING

BAIT

Crabs can usually be tempted out of their hiding places by offering some food; a piece of fish dangled on the end of a string will often do the trick. Hooks are not necessary, because the crab will hold on very tightly once it has found the bait and can be hauled out of the water. Try offering different types of bait to find out which they prefer. If the bait is left in position for a long time, more timid creatures may come to investigate, so don't pull it out immediately if there is no response at first. Fish may show more interest if it is held just below the surface, while prawns may find it if it is held nearer to the bottom or the sides of a gulley. Sometimes small fish and prawns hover around a feeding crab, hoping to catch scraps of food.

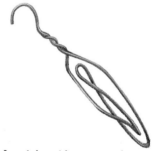

A metal coat hanger can be twisted to form a hook with a long handle; wrap string around the handle to make it easier to grip. Use the hook to coax crabs gently out of crevices between rocks.

Drop net ▽

This has a circular frame with a weight in, so that it drops to the bottom. The rope has floats on it so it can be held vertically in the water. Bait is put in the net's centre to attract fish or prawns.

Shrimp net ▽

A shrimp net has one straight edge so that it can be pushed along the bottom. The straight edge needs to be made of wood so that it is not damaged by rocks as it is used, and the pole needs to be very strong.

Circular net ▷

A circular net is used for searching amongst seaweeds in deep pools and it, too, needs a strong pole.

PROJECT

Investigate the layers in a large rock pool by using different nets. The bottom of the pool may have a layer of shells and pebbles on it; use the shrimp net to scoop up some of this material and examine it in a shallow dish. Watch the shells carefully, as some may have the original molluscs in them, whilst others will have been taken over as homes by hermit crabs (right). The sweep net will be ideal for catching fish living in the weedier parts of the pool. It should be swept through the weeds with an upwards motion to dislodge any fish which are hiding there. Allow the water to drain away before attempting to lift the net out.

NOTES AND PHOTOGRAPHY

It is very important to make accurate notes of your findings on the seashore. Get into the habit of carrying a notebook and pencil with you each time you visit the shore, and write down the date, the time of day of your visit, and the times of high and low tides. Use a map to check the exact location of the shore you are working on and check its name. The weather and sea conditions should also be noted. You may spot a creature or plant which you can identify and which cannot be removed from the shore. Make a sketch of these and note down their size, colourings and any movements they make – it will be much easier for you to identify them later when you look in a reference book. Your notes will make a useful record of your work.

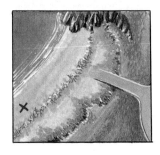

When you see a plant or creature, make a sketch of its location – you might want to look for it another day. Note which part of the shore it is on, and show where it was seen in relation to fixed features such as paths.

Most marine creatures and plants look best under water, so use a small clear plastic container to observe them and note down any special movements you see. Some containers are made with a magnifying glass as a lid and a centimetre scale marked out on the base.

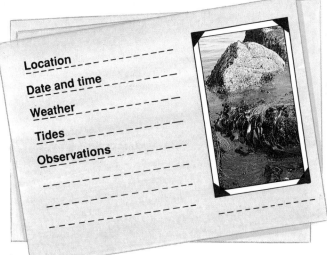

Location _ _ _ _ _ _ _ _ _ _
Date and time _ _ _ _ _ _ _
Weather _ _ _ _ _ _ _ _ _ _
Tides _ _ _ _ _ _ _ _ _ _ _ _
Observations _ _ _ _ _ _ _
_ _ _ _ _ _ _ _ _ _ _ _ _ _ _ _
_ _ _ _ _ _ _ _ _ _   _ _ _ _ _ _

Photographs make an excellent record of your visit to the shore. By taking photographs you will not need to remove specimens. Always write the details of the subject on the photographs and file them in an organised way.

PHOTOGRAPHY

Salt water will badly damage a camera so take a cloth with you to wipe your hands before you touch it. Use a tripod to hold the camera steady, as the seashore can be windy and the ground is uneven. A close-up lens is best for photographing most marine organisms. Many can be photographed where you find them, but some will look best if they are placed on a plain background such as sand; always return them to their original home when you have finished with them. A small shallow tray will enable you to place delicate creatures in salt water against a clear background. Try photographing the shore at half-hourly intervals to show the changing tides.

SANDY AND MUDDY SHORES

Many creatures will be very difficult to see as they spend most of their lives buried beneath the sand or mud. As the tide falls, look at the surface for signs of activity; there may be tracks, casts or breathing tubes on the surface, and these will show that there may be creatures underneath. Filter some sand or mud through a gardener's sieve; but smaller creatures may still escape, so a small sample of sand could be placed in a bucket of salt water and stirred gently – creatures present will be dislodged.

Quicksand
Quicksand can be a danger on some shores, but hazardous areas are usually indicated by warning signs. Wide sandy bays with shallow creeks running across them seem to be the worst. If you are unlucky and fall into quicksand, it is important to move slowly and spread your weight.

The strand line on a sandy shore collects many of the creatures which live buried in the sand. Look for the empty shells of urchins and molluscs. Gulls scavenge on the strand line, especially after storms.

Groynes are built to prevent the sand from shifting along the beach. Tides and currents deposit many creatures alongside the groynes, and some make their homes on them.

On very exposed sandy beaches, large pools can form as the sea scours the beach. Many fish get stranded in them as the tide falls and they can be caught in a shrimp net. Tiny sand gobies and prawns lie partly buried in the sand; try making a shadow over the pool to watch how they move. Beware of soft sand in some pools.

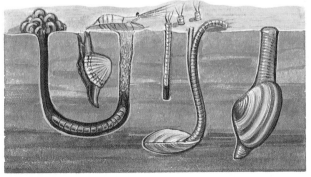

The inhabitants of sandy and muddy beaches all live at different levels. Some are so deep that they need special feeding and breathing tubes to reach the surface. Try digging a pit in the mud, and look at the sides of the pit to find the creatures living at their own levels. Dig out some shell-fish to watch how they burrow back.

ROCKY SHORES

To view under water, use a viewing pail (such as this clear-bottomed container) or wear a diving mask.

GENERAL TECHNIQUES

Try to visit just before low tide. Approach carefully, because there may be seabirds, some waiting for the tide to recede completely. Begin at the bottom of the beach, and work upwards so that you do not get cut off by the incoming tide. Most inhabitants will be found in damp areas, but species such as limpets avoid drying out by clamping tightly to rocks, thus reducing water loss. Always be careful on rocks, especially those that are wet or have a slippery seaweed covering.

Rock pools
Small, shallow rock pools high on the shore soon heat up when exposed to the sun, losing oxygen and becoming more salty as they slowly evaporate. Therefore they are not colonised by many creatures. Look in the larger, shadier pools, which have conditions similar to those of the sea.

Investigate rock crevices  for molluscs, and shallow water at the base of rocks for anemones and starfish. Jelly blobs (right) are anemones which have retracted their tentacles until the tide returns – these are beadlet anemones in a sea cave. Some species such as crabs are well camouflaged, so wait a while in case movement gives a creature away.

Many marine animals  hide beneath seaweed. Use a stick to reach seaweed not exposed by the tide, and seach carefully among the fronds. Small creatures can be found under rocks, too. When you have looked under rocks and stones, replace them as you found them.

Remain crouched and ▷ quiet and do not break the skyline when scanning the rocks for wildlife. You may need to wait patiently.

HOW TO WATCH

Scan out at sea and on the shore for birds, such as these small turnstones. Look for sunbathing or swimming seals, too. Down at the shoreline there may be some drifting jellyfish or small fish. When looking into rock pools, sit quietly with your face to the sun, to avoid casting shadows. Polaroid sun glasses will reduce the glare when you look into water.

SAFETY ON THE SHORE

Always take care when visiting the seashore. The strand line may be littered with dangerous objects, especially if there is a busy harbour or sea-lane nearby. It is a good idea to wear plimsolls for paddling and walking on the sand because of the danger of stepping on broken glass or rusty metal; this will also prevent your skin from being contaminated with oil. Sometimes canisters of dangerous chemicals are washed up; these should not be touched. In sunny weather there is a danger of sunburn; the clear air and the sea-breeze can lead to severe sunburn, so wear a hat if you are out during the middle of the day and apply plenty of sun-cream. Also, take a first-aid kit with you.

Always consult your local tide timetables before going on to the shore. Try to visit as the tide is falling so that you have time to work before the tide comes in.

Beaches which are easily accessible at low tide may be completely cut off at high tide, so check carefully for your return route before visiting them. Always keep an eye on the tide and your watch, making sure that you have plenty of time left before the tide is high.

high tide

low tide

Beaches which are unsafe ▷ for swimming may be marked by red flags – do not enter the water.

CODE OF CONDUCT

Sometimes the wave action at the base of a cliff can be very strong, so in areas where there are warning notices it is dangerous to get too close to the water. Do not trespass when going to the shore, and keep to footpaths. Litter, particularly glass bottles, can hurt wildlife and other visitors. It is easy to disturb nesting birds (right), so always approach likely nesting areas carefully. Replace rocks, plants and creatures you find on the shore, just as you found them, and in the same place.

MAKING A SHELL COLLECTION

Shells are common objects on the strand line; in some places they form large shell banks. They may be of a single species, or they may be of a great variety with many species occurring on the same beach. Large sandy beaches with rocks offshore are often very good collecting areas. Never collect live shells; it is not necessary to kill molluscs in order to take their shells. Always check that the shells you remove are empty, and that they are not inhabited by hermit crabs or other creatures. Keep a record of the place and date of collection of the shells, and label each specimen with its name.

Store the shells ▷ carefully, keeping related species together. They can be held on to card by small spots of glue or placed in small compartments.

Some shells will be clean when you find them, having been bleached by the sun and worn smooth by sand. After a storm you may find shells with the dead animal inside. Clean these gently in warm soapy water and don't boil them. Shells with barnacles or tube worms on can be interesting, too.

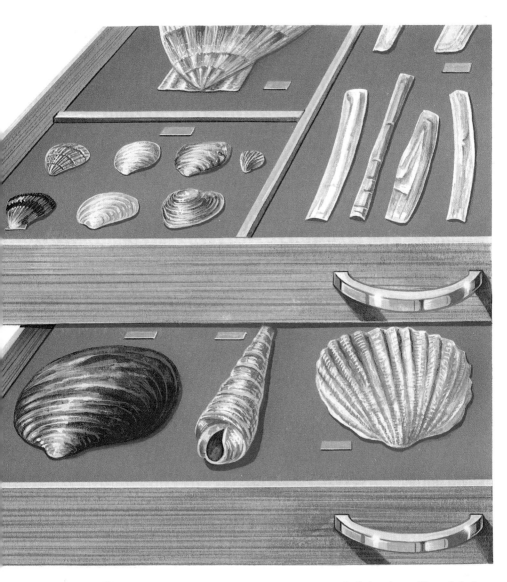

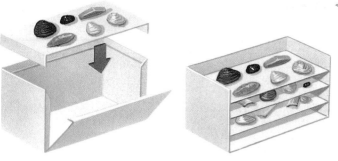

A shoe box with card shelves in it will make a good home for a collection of small shells. Glue them on to the card and label them. If possible collect two or more specimens of each shell so that both sides can be displayed, and any colour or size variations among them can be illustrated.

SHELTERED ROCKY SHORES

The dense growth of seaweeds which can
develop on a sheltered rocky shore provides the
ideal habitat for many marine creatures. When
the tide is out the thick blanket of weed
protects them from predators or from the heat
of the sun, and when the tide is in the
seaweeds float upwards, creating an
underwater forest in which fish, crabs, prawns
and molluscs can search for their food. Some
delicate species can grow to a great size.

Serrated wrack
Serrated wrack grows on the
middle shore and forms thick
blankets which hide more
delicate creatures.

Mussels
Mussels grow in large
colonies on exposed rocks
and filter the seawater to
obtain food.

Kelp bed
Kelps are uncovered only by
the lowest tides and are
unable to survive for
long out of water.

Bladder wrack
Bladder wrack floats
upwards as the tide comes
in, and allows small
organisms to hide while
they feed.

Flat periwinkle
The flat periwinkle looks like
the bladders on bladder
wrack, on which it is
commonly found.

As the tide rises, the ▷ gas-filled bladders lift the seaweeds up, and fish, such as this 15-spined stickleback, begin to swim amongst them. Some fish look like the seaweeds and are very difficult to spot.

Lomentaria articulata
This seaweed grows best where the rocks are sheltered, and it can also grow where there are overhangs.

Irish moss
Irish moss is an edible seaweed which is collected for food in some places.

Knotted wrack
Knotted wrack reaches a great size in very sheltered places and has extra large gas bladders.

Breadcrumb sponge
Sheltered areas of rock below seaweeds are safe places for sponges to grow.

Sea scorpion
Sea scorpions lurk in sheltered spots waiting for an unwary fish or shrimp to get close enough to catch.

Common limpet
On sheltered shores limpets can grow to a great size; they feed on the young stages of seaweeds.

ROCK POOLS

Rock pools are home to a variety of marine organisms normally found in deep water. Large pools allow fish to survive above the low-water mark, and beadlet anemones and prawns feed on tiny creatures stranded in the pools by the falling tide. Very shallow pools become too hot for many creatures in summer, but they are home to encrusting pink seaweeds, top shells and limpets. Delicate green and red seaweeds may shelter tiny molluscs and sea slugs.

Lithophyllum incrustans
This forms pink patches in shallow pools, and feels like chalk when it is dry.

Corallina officinalis
This has a jointed stem and forms quite dense tufts in sheltered pools.

Flat top shell
Flat top shells feed in tiny pools on very small algae.

Limpet
Limpets feed on algae in shallow pools.

Shore crab
Shore crabs are very common and can easily be seen in pools as they search for food. Larger crabs sometimes hide under stones or seaweed.

Beadlet anemone
When the tide is out, anemones close up, but if they are in a pool they can continue feeding with their tentacles open.

Sea lettuce
Pools with plenty of light are the best places for sea lettuce to grow; it is a favourite food of limpets.

Common prawn
Prawns search the bottom of pools for tiny scraps of food, but they must avoid being caught by fish.

Codium tomentosum
This forms thick tufts in deep pools and often hides small molluscs which, too, are green.

Butterfly blenny
Butterfly blennies usually live in deeper water, but will often be found stranded in pools at low tide.

EXPOSED ROCKY SHORES

The violent wave action which is a feature of exposed shores permits only the toughest of marine organisms to grow. Seaweeds are stunted and molluscs must anchor themselves firmly to the rocks. Limpets clamp down tightly when waves break over them, whilst mussels fix themselves to the rock with tough threads. Acorn barnacles can withstand a heavy pounding, and are sometimes the most abundant creatures. Only lichens can grow in the splash zone above the high-water mark.

Channelled wrack
Channelled wrack grows high up on the shore and is able to cope with long periods out of the water.

Black lichen
The black lichen is sometimes so common that the rocks look as if they are covered with tar.

Bladder wrack
In very rough places, bladder wrack forms only quite small plants with few bladders.

Dabberlocks
Dabberlocks can grow in very rough water, but cannot survive in the air for long.

Orange lichen
Orange lichens can grow on rocks which are splashed by salt water.

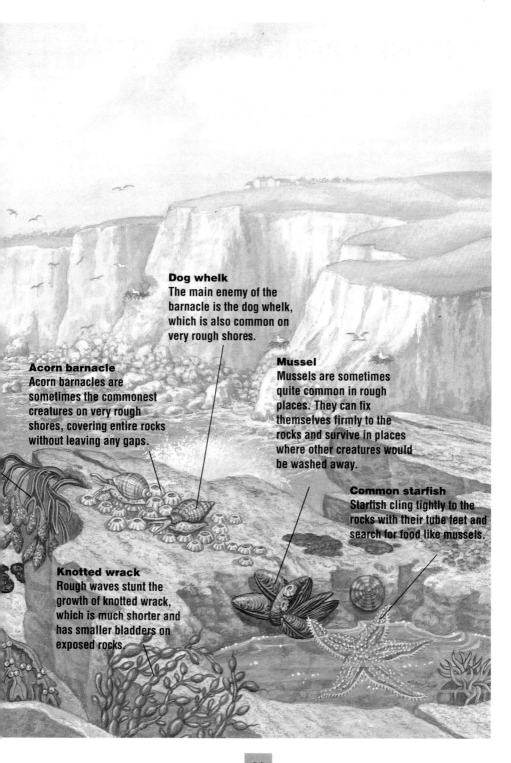

Dog whelk
The main enemy of the barnacle is the dog whelk, which is also common on very rough shores.

Acorn barnacle
Acorn barnacles are sometimes the commonest creatures on very rough shores, covering entire rocks without leaving any gaps.

Mussel
Mussels are sometimes quite common in rough places. They can fix themselves firmly to the rocks and survive in places where other creatures would be washed away.

Common starfish
Starfish cling tightly to the rocks with their tube feet and search for food like mussels.

Knotted wrack
Rough waves stunt the growth of knotted wrack, which is much shorter and has smaller bladders on exposed rocks.

SANDY SHORES

At first sight there seems to be nothing alive on a sandy shore, but most of its life is hidden. Clues can be found on the surface in the form of casts or depressions made by feeding or breathing activities. Many creatures live buried in the sand and emerge only to feed at high tide. Fish advance with the rising tide to catch worms and molluscs emerging from their burrows, and wading birds run along the water's edge looking for movement in the sand.

Sanderling
Sanderlings are long-distance migrants which stop on the shore to feed on tiny organisms disturbed by waves.

Masked crab
Only a tiny depression in the sand reveals where the masked crab is hidden; it rarely comes to the surface.

Lugworm
The coils of sand and small depressions show where the V-shaped burrow of the lugworm lies.

Weever fish
Partly hidden in the sand, the weever fish is a danger to paddlers because its poisonous spines can inflict a painful sting.

Tern

Terns hover over the waves looking for tiny fish and shrimps, which they can catch in quite shallow water.

PROJECT

Odd fishing is a method for catching razor shells. At low tide walk slowly backwards along the water's edge, watching for the squirt of water made as a razor shell dives deeper when it feels someone walking over it. Gently push a thin wooden rod into the depression until it touches the razor shell; when it feels this it clamps the two halves of its shell and grips hard. It can then be pulled to the surface.

Shrimp

Shrimps have almost transparent bodies, so they are very difficult to see when viewed from above.

Flounder

The flattened body of the flounder and its sandy colouring help to hide it.

Thin tellin

A tiny tube sweeping over the surface shows where the thin tellin is feeding. It scoops tiny food particles from the sand.

Pod razor shell

The powerful 'foot' of the razor shell is used to pull it rapidly down into the sand if danger threatens.

STRAND LINES

Large quantities of seaweeds, shells and other debris are thrown up on to beaches by the tide. Gulls scavenge along the strand line, and smaller birds search for sandhoppers and kelp flies beneath rotting seaweed. Empty mollusc shells, mermaid's purses and cuttlebones show which organisms live offshore, whilst oiled seabirds indicate how the sea is becoming polluted. Driftwood often contains the burrowings of shipworms or gribbles.

Kelp-fly
Rotting seaweed provides a source of food for kelp-fly larvae, which in turn provide food for birds.

Shrew
Shrews search the strand line for kelp-fly larvae and sea slaters.

Kelp
Storms often damage large kelps, which are then thrown up on to the beach by the tide. There they slowly change colour and decompose.

Sea slater
Look like giant woodlice and feed on rotting seaweed and other debris.

Turnstone
As well as flipping over stones, turnstones search amongst rotting seaweed for their food. They take many sandhoppers and kelp flies.

Drums containing ▷
chemicals are sometimes
washed up on beaches.
These should be reported to
the coastguard immediately,
but should never be handled
as the contents could be very
dangerous if they spill out.

Rock pipit
Rock pipits are skilled
at catching kelp flies and
their larvae.

Seabird
Oil pollution at sea causes
the deaths of many seabirds.
Their feathers become
clogged with oil and they are
unable to swim or feed.

Shipworm
Pieces of driftwood often
have holes bored in them by
shipworms. Sometimes the
remains of the shell can be
found lining the hole.

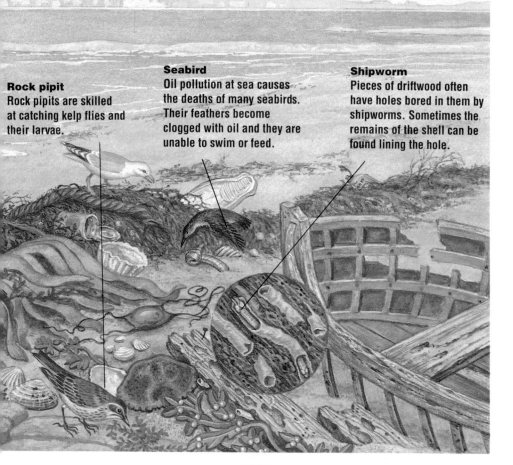

SHINGLE BEACHES

Pebbles rolled around by breaking waves make a very inhospitable place for marine organisms to live, so very few creatures are found living in or on shingle. The beach above the high-tide line is more stable and this is often a good place for birds to nest. Many of them use only a very small amount of nest material and rely on good camouflage to protect their eggs. Some plants with deep root systems are able to grow on shingle above the high-tide line. In order to protect the cliffs and stabilise the beach, groynes are built to stop the shingle drifting.

Common tern
The common tern is able to hover over the water to look for its food. Terns nest on the ground so need quiet and undisturbed places where their eggs and chicks will be safe.

Yellow horned-poppy
Stable shingle is soon colonised by the floating seeds of yellow horned-poppy.

Thrift
One of the most widespread plants around the coast, thrift flowers in early summer.

Sea holly
Commonly found on dunes, sea holly's deep roots help it survive on shingle, too.

Sea campion
Low-growing sea campion is common on cliffs and at the top of shingle banks.

As the waves pound the beach the individual pebbles are rolled over and over, gradually becoming smooth as they rub against each other. Large boulders are moved only a short distance, and small pebbles are moved more often and over a longer distance. Gradually pebbles become graded along the beach, with large pebbles staying at one end and smaller ones ending up at the other. Try walking along a shingle beach and collecting a pebble at regular intervals; are they all the same size, or do they get larger or smaller as you progress?

Seal
Look for seals resting offshore. They can sleep at sea, too.

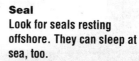

Oystercatcher
Oystercatchers roost on shingle beaches when they are not feeding, and they often nest just above the high-tide line.

Ringed plover
The black and white markings on the head make this a difficult bird to see when it is nesting on shingle.

ESTUARINE MUD

The rivers which flow into estuaries usually carry silt with them, and this is deposited as mud banks. Gradually these build up and are colonised by plants and animals, forming rich feeding grounds. Many fish live in estuaries, and some travel through them on their way to or from the sea. As the tide falls, more and more mud is exposed and birds come to feed. Herons stalk the narrow tidal creeks in search of eels and flounders, and the rare otter seeks larger prey, hunting mostly at night.

Grey heron
Herons wait patiently for a fish to come close enough to be caught.

Salmon
Salmon pass through some estuaries on their way to their spawning grounds in fast flowing rivers.

Hydrobia
Millions of these snails live on the mud of estuaries, feeding mainly on the microscopic algae. They are food for birds and fish.

Flounder
Flounders live in deep-water channels and search for crabs, shellfish and worms.

Mullet
Shoals of mullet follow the tide in, nosing their way into tiny creeks in search of food.

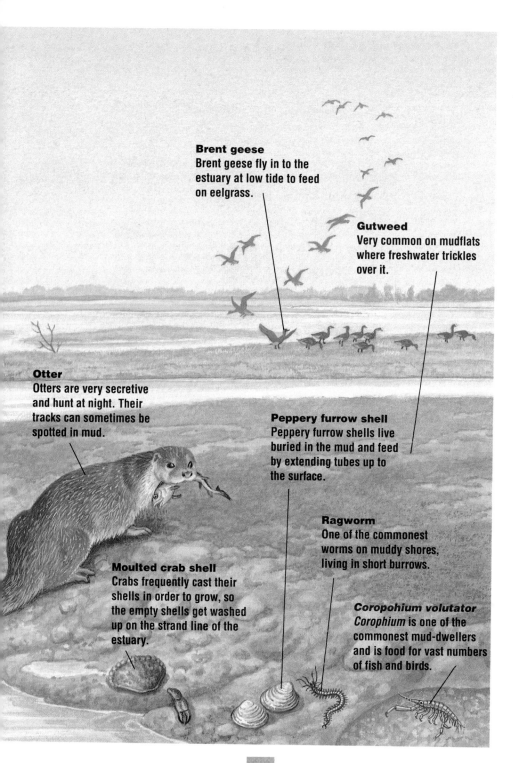

Brent geese
Brent geese fly in to the estuary at low tide to feed on eelgrass.

Gutweed
Very common on mudflats where freshwater trickles over it.

Otter
Otters are very secretive and hunt at night. Their tracks can sometimes be spotted in mud.

Peppery furrow shell
Peppery furrow shells live buried in the mud and feed by extending tubes up to the surface.

Ragworm
One of the commonest worms on muddy shores, living in short burrows.

Moulted crab shell
Crabs frequently cast their shells in order to grow, so the empty shells get washed up on the strand line of the estuary.

Coropohium volutator
Corophium is one of the commonest mud-dwellers and is food for vast numbers of fish and birds.

ESTUARINE SAND

Huge sand banks build up in some estuaries, and these make favourite hauling-out places for common seals; they spend many hours resting on the sand at low tide. Several species of mollusc live buried in the sand, where they are safe from predators and protected from the heat of the sun or from drying winds when the tide is out. Cockles are sometimes found in vast numbers, and their shells accumulate on the shore. Shrimps and sand gobies live in shallow creeks and both have colourings to match the sand; they must hide from birds such as terns and larger fish such as bass.

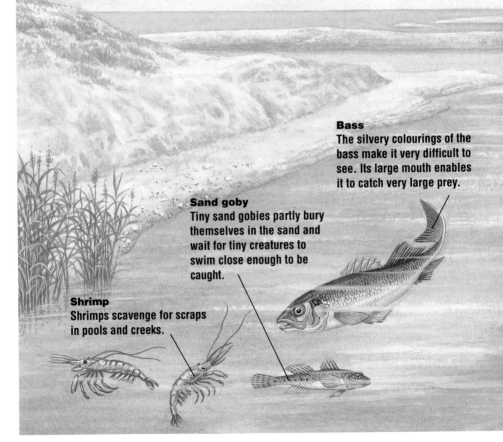

Bass
The silvery colourings of the bass make it very difficult to see. Its large mouth enables it to catch very large prey.

Sand goby
Tiny sand gobies partly bury themselves in the sand and wait for tiny creatures to swim close enough to be caught.

Shrimp
Shrimps scavenge for scraps in pools and creeks.

Cockles are so abundant ▷ in some estuaries that they are fished for and then sold as a delicacy. They are dredged up from the sea bed. Sometimes they absorb pollution from the water and cannot then be eaten.

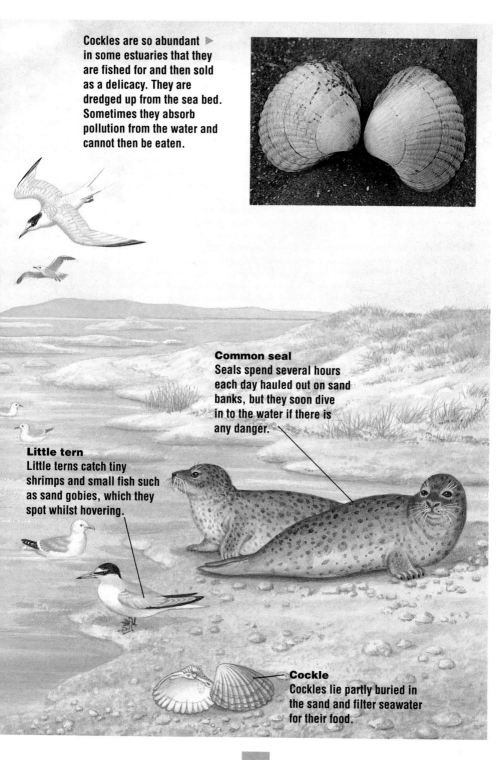

Common seal
Seals spend several hours each day hauled out on sand banks, but they soon dive in to the water if there is any danger.

Little tern
Little terns catch tiny shrimps and small fish such as sand gobies, which they spot whilst hovering.

Cockle
Cockles lie partly buried in the sand and filter seawater for their food.

SALTMARSHES

In very sheltered conditions in the upper reaches of estuaries and large bays, silt is deposited to form extensive mud banks. These are soon colonised by saltmarsh plants which are able to tolerate salt water around their roots. The plants grow in distinct zones according to how well they can cope with salt water. Tiny creeks form in the saltmarsh and these form rich feeding grounds for wading birds and gulls. Many invertebrates live in the mud, and shore crabs are common scavengers. Saltmarshes are easily damaged by severe storms or floods, and take many years to become re-colonised if plants are removed.

Sea lavender
Saltmarshes are very colourful in summer when sea lavender blooms: it often attracts butterflies.

Saltmarsh rushes
The seeds of saltmarsh rushes are important food for birds in winter.

Shore crab
Shore crabs live in holes in the sides of saltmarsh creeks and scavenge when the tide comes in.

Eelgrass
Eelgrass is one of the few flowering plants which can grow in salt water. Brent geese are fond of eating it.

Large numbers of ▷ apparently dead shore crabs are washed up on saltmarshes at very high tides, and the strand line is often covered with hundreds of shells. On closer examination they will be seen to be empty shells: the result of crabs moulting their old shells in order to grow a new one.

Sea purslane
Sea purslane is one of the commonest plants on saltmarshes. It penetrates deep into the mud.

Cord-grass
Huge areas of cord-grass grow on mudflats and protect them from erosion, allowing more delicate plants to grow below them.

Redshank
Redshanks are able to wade in shallow water and catch tiny invertebrates living in the mud. They are most numerous in winter.

Glasswort or marsh samphire
Glasswort is very tolerant of salt water and is one of the first plants to colonise new mudflats.

41

HARBOURS AND DOCKS

Harbours and docks are busy places where fish from the open sea may be landed. There is often the chance to study deep-water fish which are never encountered on the seashore. Other objects such as urchins, starfish and sponges may also be brought ashore with the catch. Some seashore plants and animals are able to colonise harbour walls if the sea is not too polluted – there may be some rocky-shore species growing in the sheltered conditions of the harbour.

Herring gull
Gulls scavenge on fish scraps and follow fishing boats. They often roost and nest on dockside buildings.

Edible crab
Crabs also enter lobster pots and are a popular delicacy in seaside restaurants.

Lobster
Lobster pots are baited with fish and then dropped into very deep water; fishermen check them frequently.

Conger eel
Large eels often live in old wrecks and are caught by deep-sea fishermen.

Skate
The fins, or 'wings', of skate are removed to be eaten, and the body often left for gulls.

Lesser spotted dogfish
Dogfish look unpleasant but they are skinned and sold by fishmongers as rock salmon.

Mackerel
One of the most popular fish is the mackerel, caught in large numbers close to the shore in late summer.

PIERS AND JETTIES

In areas where there are no natural rock outcrops, man-made structures often provide the only anchorage for species which normally live on rocky shores. Wooden piers are sometimes damaged by burrowing organisms such as shipworms, and most exposed surfaces are colonised by algae and encrusting organisms. The strong currents which sweep past piers bring a constant supply of food to filter-feeding organisms such as sponges and limpets. The seaweeds which colonise the pier supports provide safe feeding places for fish which would be exposed to danger in the sea.

Wrasse
Wrasse have narrow but muscular bodies, a spiny dorsal fin, thick lips, and powerful teeth and jaws.

Black goby
Black gobies can tolerate brackish water and live over sand, and so are often found near piers.

Red gurnard
The pectoral fins of the gurnard help it to find its food in murky water over sandy sea beds, and it can be caught by pier anglers.

Some piers are very long ▶ and allow anglers to reach fish which live in deep water – such as this father lasher, or sea scorpion. These fish often take up territories in safe hiding places beneath the pier's supports; they are attracted by the good feeding and safe hiding places.

Beadlet anemone
A constant supply of food is swept past the anemones as waves break around the pier. At low tide they close up.

Periwinkle and limpet
Several species of periwinkle can live on piers and jetties, grazing on the algae and hiding in crevices. Limpets can live in the stormiest places, so they are easily able to hold on as waves swirl around pier supports.

Five-bearded rockling
Rocklings find their food in muddy conditions, using sensitive barbels (feelers) on the head.

GREEN SEAWEEDS

GENERAL FEATURES

Green seaweeds contain a green pigment called chlorophyll which traps sunlight to help the plant make its food – a process called photosynthesis, found in all green plants.

HABITATS

Most green seaweeds live in places where they get plenty of sunlight, and are often efficient at colonising new habitats. They are even able to grow on sand and mud, in places where other larger seaweeds would get washed away by the current. They are important food plants for grazing molluscs such as limpets and periwinkles. Gutweed is very tolerant of pollution and is sometimes the only seaweed to grow on polluted shores.

Look closely at a frond of gutweed through a lens. Place a frond in a dish of water, stick a pin in one of the swollen sections and watch what happens. How do the swollen sections form?

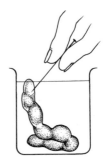

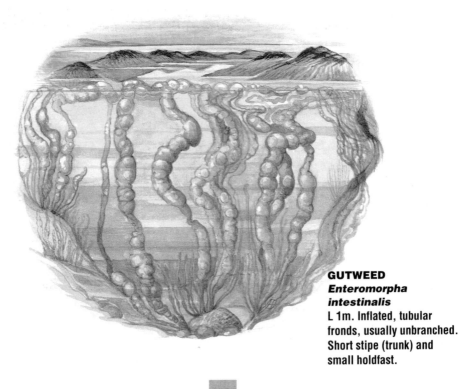

GUTWEED
Enteromorpha intestinalis
L 1m. Inflated, tubular fronds, usually unbranched. Short stipe (trunk) and small holdfast.

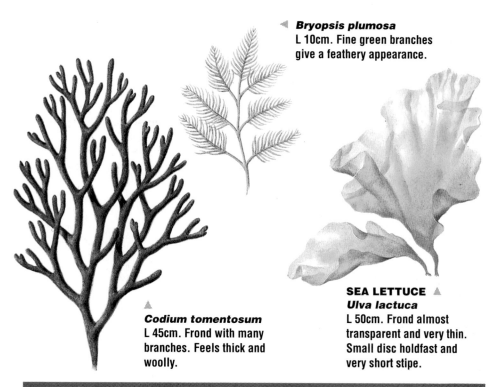

Bryopsis plumosa
L 10cm. Fine green branches
give a feathery appearance.

Codium tomentosum
L 45cm. Frond with many
branches. Feels thick and
woolly.

SEA LETTUCE ▲
Ulva lactuca
L 50cm. Frond almost
transparent and very thin.
Small disc holdfast and
very short stipe.

HOW TO WATCH

Green seaweeds need plenty of
light, so look for them in sunny
pools, on the south side of
breakwaters and groynes, and
nearer to the high-tide line. Some
species can tolerate brackish water,
so look in places where a stream
runs across a beach, or where a
waterfall tumbles down a cliff.
Many green seaweeds are very
delicate and easily damaged by
storms, so look on the strand line
after a gale and check through the
debris for washed-up specimens.
Beware of confusing red and
brown seaweeds which have
started to lose some of their
colouring in the sun. Illustrated
are gutweed (top) and sea lettuce.

WRACKS

HABITATS

Wracks are usually the commonest seaweeds on a rocky shore, in some sheltered bays forming a complete blanket over the rocks, hiding other seaweeds and marine organisms beneath them. Some float freely in sheltered saltmarshes or long sea-lochs.

GENERAL FEATURES

Wracks can live in shadier places than many green seaweeds because they can trap more light energy. Wracks produce a mucilage which makes them very slippery to walk on; this helps them to retain moisture when the tide is out. Millions of tiny reproductive cells are released into the water; these are important food for plankton feeders.

Attached to egg wrack is a small tufted red seaweed, *Polysiphonia*, which seems never to grow anywhere else. The small red seaweed does not harm its host, but grows on the outside of it.

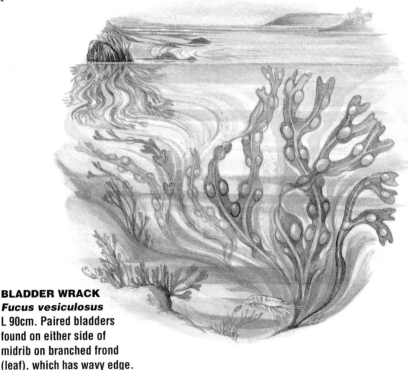

BLADDER WRACK
Fucus vesiculosus
L 90cm. Paired bladders found on either side of midrib on branched frond (leaf), which has wavy edge.

SERRATED WRACK ▽
Fucus serratus
L 160cm. Flattened fronds
with serrated edges and
swollen tips. Branched
holdfast.

KNOTTED OR △
EGG WRACK
Ascophyllum nodosum
L 150cm. Frond flattened
with slightly serrated edge,
large, single bladders,
sultana-like reproductive
bodies.

SPIRAL OR FLAT
WRACK ▷
Fucus spiralis
L 50cm. Flat fronds with
spiral twist, swollen tips and
no bladders.

PEACOCK'S TAIL ▽
Padina pavonia
L 12cm. Short stipe and
fan-shaped frond with chalky
encrustation.

CHANNEL WRACK △
Pelvetia canaliculata
L 15cm. Fronds branched
and inrolled to form channel.
Upper shore only.

KELPS

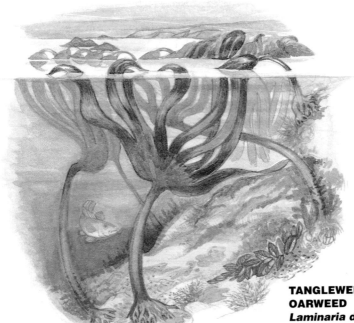

**TANGLEWEED OR
OARWEED**
Laminaria digitata
L 2m. Large tangled holdfast,
and smooth and very flexible
oval stipe with broad frond.

GENERAL FEATURES

Kelps are the largest of all seaweeds. Many of
them overwinter as a small tough holdfast and
stipe, and then produce a very large
reproductive stage in summer. When the
autumn gales blow, the reproductive stage is
ripped away and washed up on the shore,
sometimes forming huge deposits.

HABITATS

Kelps grow at the low-water mark and down
into much deeper water. The underwater kelp
forests are valuable breeding and feeding
grounds for many fish and invertebrates, and
make one of the richest habitats on the
seashore. Kelps can withstand only a short
length of time out of water, so are found only
near the low-tide line.

The holdfasts of the large
kelps make excellent hiding
places for small creatures,
some of which are rarely
found anywhere else.
A green ragworm and a
small green mussel are most
common in holdfasts.

SUGAR KELP OR POOR MAN'S WEATHER GLASS
Laminaria saccharina
L 4m. Branched holdfast, short smooth stipe and wrinkled frond.

SEA OAK OR PODWEED ▷
Halidrys siliquosa
L 1.5m. Alternate branches and long, pointed air bladders (pods).

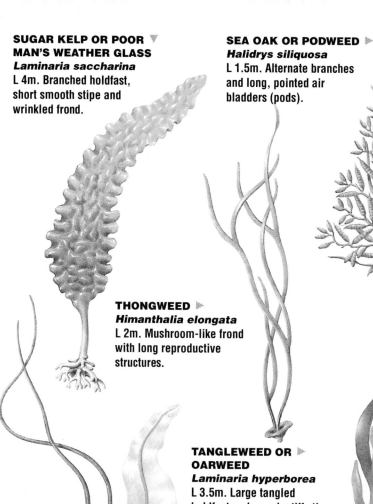

THONGWEED ▷
Himanthalia elongata
L 2m. Mushroom-like frond with long reproductive structures.

TANGLEWEED OR OARWEED ▷
Laminaria hyperborea
L 3.5m. Large tangled holdfast and round, stiff stipe tapering towards frond.

SEA BOOTLACE OR MERMAID'S FISHING LINES
Chorda filum
L 8m. Unbranched, slimy frond, often mixed with other marine algae.

FURBELOWS ▷
Sacchorhiza polyschides
L 4m. Huge, warty, bulbous holdfast and flattened frond.

RED SEAWEEDS

HABITATS

Red seaweeds contain a red pigment which hides the green chlorophyll. They are able to live in quite low light, and so are often found below other seaweeds, in shady gulleys and quite deep water. Most are found on the lower shore, but some live higher up if there is shade or very sheltered conditions.

GENERAL FEATURES

Most red seaweeds are small and delicate, and are seen at their best only when floating in water. They make excellent pressed specimens. When washed up after storms they quickly lose their red pigments, becoming green then finally white, so these specimens are not an accurate guide to the living plants.

The holdfast of *Laminaria hyperborea* is rough, and red seaweeds are able to fix themselves to it. Look at washed-up laminarians to find deep-water red seaweeds which are normally out of reach.

IRISH MOSS OR CARRAGHEEN
Chondrus crispus
L 15cm. Flattened branched frond. In water, seems to change colour.

LAYER
Porphyra umbilicalis
L 30cm. Feels like polythene.
Becomes darker when dry.

Phycodrys rubens ▷
L 35cm. Delicate oak-leaf-like fronds with mid-rib and veins.

PEPPER DULSE ▲
Laurencia pinnatifida
L 20cm. Frond branched and flattened, purplish to greenish.

Rhodymenia palmata ▽
(Palmaria palmata)
L 30cm. Disc holdfast, flattened frond with leaflets on edges.

Corallina officinalis ▲
L 15cm. Segmented like a tiny skeleton, bleaches in sunlight.

◁ **DULSE**
Dilsea carnosa
L 30cm. Disc holdfast and flattened, torn fronds.

53

LICHENS

GENERAL FEATURES

Lichens are non-flowering plants which are formed from a fungus and an alga. The fungus forms the body of the lichen and the alga gives it its colour. Some grow as only the thinnest of encrustations on bare rocks, whilst others are more leafy and develop into quite large plants. The central surface often has circular disc-like reproductive bodies on it. Lichens are very slow-growing, and very intolerant of pollution, so they are good indicators of air purity.

HABITATS

On very exposed shores, they are often the only plants above the high-tide line because of their tolerance of salt water. Each species has its own level of tolerance, so they live at different levels on the shore.

Using a hand lens, look closely at the edge of a lichen to see the growing tips. Examine the central region (or thallus) to see the reproductive bodies, which are often a different colour. Study the areas where two lichens of the same or different species meet to see if they overlap or grow together.

Caloplaca marina
L 10cm. Forms rounded colonies of many small lobes, with yellowish-orange body and reddish fruiting bodies.

SEA IVORY
Ramalina siliquosa
D 5cm. Erect or hanging.
Warty surface.

PROJECT

Look at an exposed shore from a distance and see how the lichens are arranged in zones or bands. Which colour is nearest the high-water mark, and which is furthest from it? Identify the species. Do they grow where rocks are shaded by overhangs or only in sunny places?

Anaptychia fusca ▲
D 10cm. Brownish, with many lobes and darker fruiting bodies.

Xanthoria parietina
D 10cm. Curled edges and dead centre in old plants. Mostly orange.

Lecanora atra ▲
D 8cm. Greyish, with black fruiting bodies.

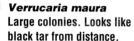

Verrucaria maura
Large colonies. Looks like black tar from distance.

ROCKY-SHORE PLANTS

GENERAL FEATURES

Flowering plants which grow on a rocky shore must be very tolerant of salt spray and stormy conditions. Most rocky-shore plants have small leaves which are waxy or fleshy to save water, and many of them also have strong roots to penetrate narrow crevices. They have to grow where there is very little soil and fresh water.

HABITATS

No flowering plants grow below the high-tide line on a rocky shore; most grow above the splash zone. In winter they may be drenched by salt spray, but in summer they may experience a drought. A further problem is the droppings of seabirds nesting on cliffs above the shore line.

THRIFT OR SEA PINK
Armeria maritima
H 30cm. Narrow but fleshy leaves form a cushion. Flowers many different shades of pink.

Thrift, or sea pink, is one of the plants best suited to rocky cliffs. Its deep root holds the plant down and collects fresh water, and the leaves form a cushion to help retain moisture.

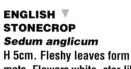

SHEEP'S-BIT ▽ SCABIOUS
Jasione montana
H 30cm. Bright blue flowers, may creep over bare rocks.

SEA CAMPION ▲
Silene maritima
H 25cm. Flowers white with inflated bladder, leaves oval.

ENGLISH ▽ **STONECROP**
Sedum anglicum
H 5cm. Fleshy leaves form mats. Flowers white, star-like.

ROCK SEA SPURREY ▲
Spergularia rupicola
L 30cm. Dense patches. Flowers pink, leaves sticky.

ROCK SAMPHIRE ▲
Crithmum maritimum
L 45cm. Leaves fleshy, flowers creamy-yellow.

PROJECT

Watch plants in flower on sunny days to see which insects visit them. The green tiger beetle (illustrated) may try to catch other insects visiting flowers. The thrift clearwing moth lays its eggs on thrift and sea plantain.

SALTMARSH PLANTS

**MARSH SAMPHIRE
OR GLASSWORT**
Salicornia europaea
H 20cm. Fleshy stems and
branches in segments, green
at first, but reddening in
late summer.

HABITATS

Saltmarsh plants are able to colonise the mud
and make it more stable. As more and more
plants grow on the mud the level begins to rise
owing to sediment collecting around the roots.
Gradually the saltmarsh becomes drier, and
only the very highest tides, or sudden floods,
cover it with salt water. Narrow creeks running
through saltmarshes are sometimes very deep,
with little growing in them, but their banks
are firmer and have more plants on them.

GENERAL FEATURES

Some saltmarsh plants can tolerate long periods
under salt water, so they grow nearest to the
water, whilst others can cope with only a short
period underwater, so they grow further away.
Most of them have very extensive root systems
to hold them in the mud and waxy leaves to
cut down on water loss.

The tiny snail *Hydrobia* is
sometimes very common in
saltmarshes and can be
found by looking at the stems
of plants such as glasswort
at low tide. It climbs up them
to graze on minute algae.

CORDGRASS
Spartina townsendii
H 1m. Tough grass, upright stems. Has yellowish flower-heads.

PROJECT

In late summer, when sea lavender is in flower, it attracts large numbers of insects, including butterflies. Some of these will be migrants, having travelled across the sea to reach this country, so the sea lavender will be the first source of nectar they come to. Watch saltmarsh plants to see which insects visit them.

SEA PURSLANE ▷
Halimione portulacoides
H 80cm. Covers huge areas. Leaves greyish and mealy, flowers yellow.

◁ GREATER SEA SPURREY
Spergularia media
L 30cm. Flowers white or pink-tipped, leaves narrow.

SEA LAVENDER ▷
Limonium vulgare
H 35cm. Long-stalked oval leaves, lavender flowers. Does not have a scent.

EELGRASS ▽
Zostera marina
L 50cm. Grass-like leaves, tiny flowers. Lower shore.

DUNE AND STRAND-LINE PLANTS

HABITATS

Sand dunes are very difficult places for plants to grow in because of the shifting sand and lack of water and nutrients.

GENERAL FEATURES

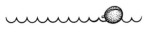

Most sand-dune plants have very long and branching roots which can penetrate far into the sand to find water and hold the plant down. Their leaves are usually waxy and reduced in size to retain water. When plants colonise sand dunes they provide suitable conditions for more delicate plants and tiny animals to live there as well.

The floating seeds of strand-line plants drift for many miles. Some will end up in unsuitable places and fail to grow, and some will be eaten by birds on the strand line elsewhere. Only a few will survive.

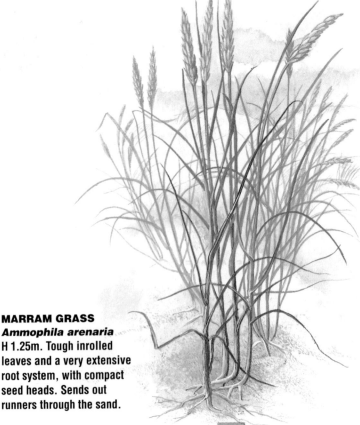

MARRAM GRASS
Ammophila arenaria
H 1.25m. Tough inrolled leaves and a very extensive root system, with compact seed heads. Sends out runners through the sand.

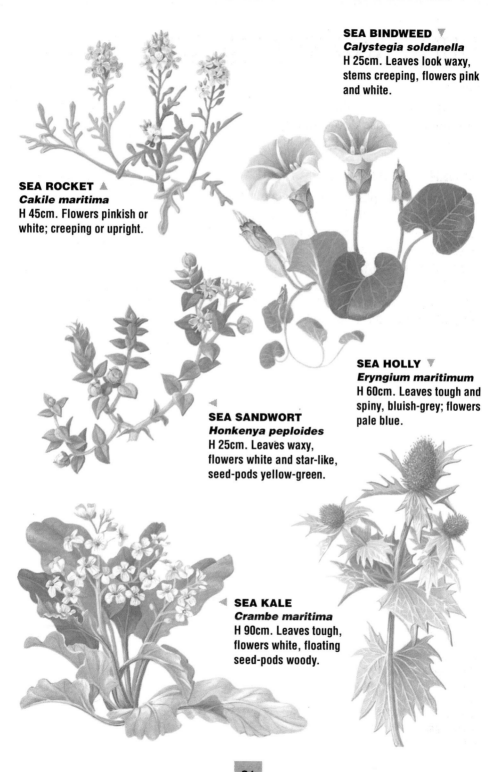

SEA BINDWEED ▼
Calystegia soldanella
H 25cm. Leaves look waxy,
stems creeping, flowers pink
and white.

SEA ROCKET ▲
Cakile maritima
H 45cm. Flowers pinkish or
white; creeping or upright.

SEA HOLLY ▼
Eryngium maritimum
H 60cm. Leaves tough and
spiny, bluish-grey; flowers
pale blue.

◄ **SEA SANDWORT**
Honkenya peploides
H 25cm. Leaves waxy,
flowers white and star-like,
seed-pods yellow-green.

◄ **SEA KALE**
Crambe maritima
H 90cm. Leaves tough,
flowers white, floating
seed-pods woody.

SPONGES

BREADCRUMB SPONGE
Halichondria panicea
Forms large encrusting
patches, often green, but
may be orange, brown or
white in colour.

GENERAL FEATURES

Sponges are simple animals which feed by
filtering seawater and extracting tiny organisms
from it. Water is drawn in through many tiny
pores on the surface. When it has been filtered
it is passed out through a single larger pore.
The body has no definite form to it, although
the pores can be seen through a hand lens.

HABITS

Some sponges vary in colour: they rely on
microscopic algae living inside them to provide
colour. Some produce an acid and bore their
way into shells and soft rock; and some live
only in association with other animals.

Feeding
To watch sponges feeding, it
is necessary to observe them
underwater. Choose a sponge
which you can move easily
without harming it, such as
one on a small, loose rock,
and put it in a large
container of clean seawater.
Using a pipette, release a
few drops of water made
cloudy with milk or yeast
suspension near the surface
of the sponge. Watch through
a hand lens to see what
happens next.

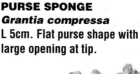
PURSE SPONGE
Grantia compressa
L 5cm. Flat purse shape with
large opening at tip.

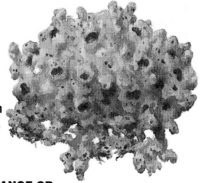

Myxilla incrustans ▷
W 15cm. Large clumps form
on stones on muddy shores,
mostly orange.

**SEA ORANGE OR
SULPHUR SPONGE** ▽
Suberites domuncula
D 25cm. Encrusts whelk
shells inhabited by hermit
crabs. Bright orange.

BORING SPONGE △
Cliona celata
D 2mm. Burrows into shells
or limestone. Yellow or
green.

HOW TO WATCH

Sponges live at all levels on the
shore but are often hidden, so look
below overhangs, and in shaded
areas below large seaweeds such as
wracks and kelps. The tangled
holdfasts of large kelps are good
sites for smaller sponges and the
purse sponge often grows on tufted
red algae. Large bivalve shells on
the strand line may have holes
bored in them by the very small
boring sponge.

HYDROZOA

GENERAL FEATURES

Hydroids are microscopic animals which form colonies. Individuals are called polyps, and they have very simple bodies. The polyps join together to form colonies in which most individuals collect food, but some are concerned with defence or reproduction. Some colonies contain very large numbers of polyps and look like pieces of tough dried seaweed.

HABITS

Their tough branching colonies look like miniature trees – they were once called 'sea firs'. They may grow on rocks, but many grow on seaweeds, particularly large kelps. After storms, large numbers of hydroids are washed up on the strand line.

Place some hydrozoa specimens in clean seawater. The feeding tentacles should soon emerge from the tiny polyps. Observe the reactions when the water is stirred and when a small object touches the tentacles.

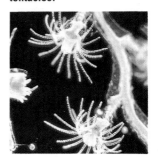

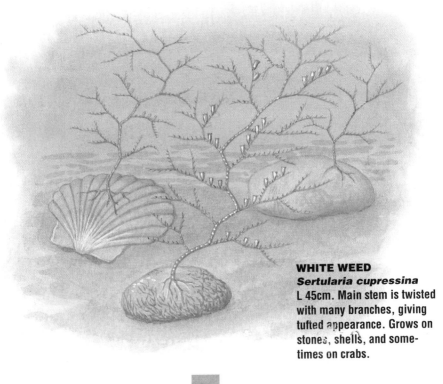

WHITE WEED
Sertularia cupressina
L 45cm. Main stem is twisted with many branches, giving tufted appearance. Grows on stones, shells, and sometimes on crabs.

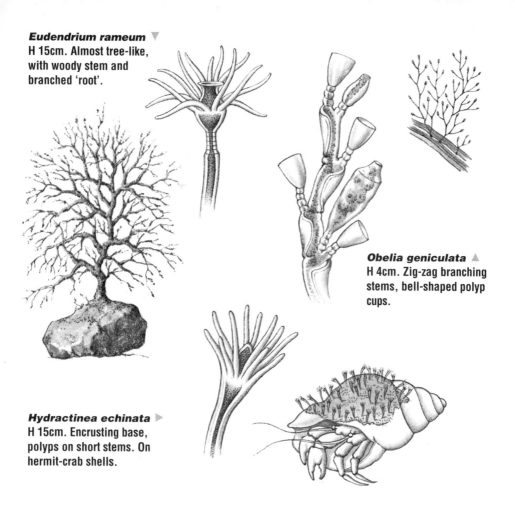

Eudendrium rameum ▽
H 15cm. Almost tree-like, with woody stem and branched 'root'.

Obelia geniculata △
H 4cm. Zig-zag branching stems, bell-shaped polyp cups.

Hydractinea echinata ▷
H 15cm. Encrusting base, polyps on short stems. On hermit-crab shells.

HOW TO WATCH

Hydroids (*Aglaophenia tubulifera* is illustrated) are plankton-feeding animals which do not need light, so they are often found in dark places such as under overhangs. They will also grow in light places such as on the fronts of wracks and benefit from the buoyancy of the plants they are living on. Dead specimens can be dried and pressed like seaweeds, and will not decay if kept in a dry place.

JELLYFISH AND SEA GOOSEBERRY

COMMON JELLYFISH
Aurelia aurita
D 25cm. Flat, saucer-shaped, with longer central tentacles and rim of short tentacles. Four violet horseshoe shapes are reproductive organs.

GENERAL FEATURES

Most jellyfish consist of a saucer-shaped jelly surrounded by trailing tentacles, which capture prey. In some species they can inflict a painful sting on human skin. One stage in the jellyfish life cycle is a small polyp fixed to a rock; this produces the free-swimming medusa which is the familiar jellyfish. The very small medusae quickly grow to reach full size.

HABITS

Jellyfish usually drift with the tides and currents, but they can swim weakly to keep near the surface. If jellyfish become stranded they cannot get back to the water and very quickly die. Sometimes jellyfish form huge shoals and can be seen from the shore – look from bridges over narrow inlets.

Jellyfish have simple bodies showing radial symmetry: that is, they could be divided into two matching halves along any line. The compass jellyfish shows this very clearly because its body has rays and quite definite lobes at the margins.

Cyanea lamarckii ▲
D 15cm. Blue and violet,
many tentacles, can inflict
painful sting.

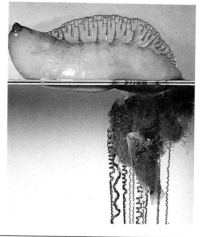

◄ **SEA GOOSEBERRY**
Pleurobrachia pileus
L 3cm. Tentacles much
longer. Not a jellyfish.
Luminous, free-swimming,
sometimes abundant.

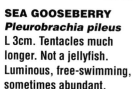

Rhizostoma pulmo ▶
D 90cm. Domed and solid-
looking, may be very
common. Tiny shrimps
sometimes live in tentacles.

COMPASS JELLYFISH ▲
Chrysaora hyoscella
D 30cm. 32 lobes and 24
tentacles around rim, four
long 'mouth arms'.

SEA ANEMONES

GENERAL FEATURES

Sea anemones are simple soft-bodied animals. The body is a cylinder with a mouth surrounded by stinging tentacles. The cylinder base is a muscular foot which anchors the anemone to the rocks, but also enables it to move from time to time. In some species microscopic algae live inside the anemone. The algae release oxygen which the anemone uses, and they use the carbon dioxide formed by the anemone – a mutually beneficial arrangement called symbiosis.

HABITATS

Some species live between tide lines and can survive for short periods out of water, but others live only in pools or below the low-water mark.

The beadlet anemone occurs in several colour forms, with red being the most common. Usually, individuals of one colour are found together. Look at pools and the sides of gulleys, under overhangs and in caves, and check all the colonies to find out if the different colour forms are mixed, or if they have a preference for a habitat or level on the shore.

BEADLET ANEMONE
Actinia equina
H 7cm, D 5cm. 24 blue spots circle the rings of tentacles. Very variable in colour and very common at most levels on the shore.

Look in shallow rock pools where there is a growth of *Corallina* seaweed for the snakelocks anemones (right). Their tentacles have iridescent tips and cannot be retracted; they move all the time. The anemones occur in two colour forms. Do the two different colours occur in the same area? Look at shady and sunny rock pools to find out about their preferences.

Beadlet anemones (left) are aggressive and fight each other for good feeding positions. Measure the distances between individuals in a colony to find out how close each will allow another anemone to settle. Try placing two anemones close together. Do not pull one off a rock; try to find ones which are on stones or shells which you can move easily. Remember, anemones move slowly, so don't expect immediate results.

SNAKELOCKS ANEMONE ▽
Anemonia viridis (sulcata)
H 10cm, D 20cm. Brown or greyish-green with iridescent tips; tentacles wave around.

GEM ANEMONE ▽
Bunodactis verrucosa
H 3cm, D 6cm. Six rows of white warts on column; pinkish, with other colours at base.

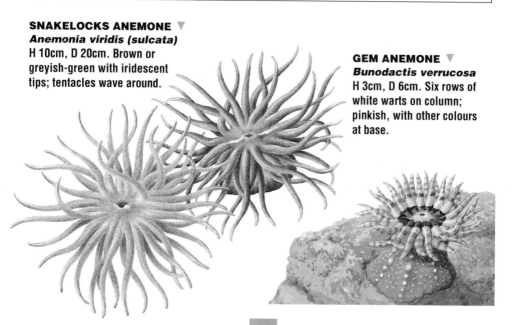

SEA ANEMONES

GENERAL FEATURES

Some of the sea anemones which live in deep
water are much bigger than those on the
shore. One reason may be that they can spend
all their time feeding, not needing to retract
their tentacles when the tide is out.

HABITATS

They are found in large numbers on the
underwater legs of piers and oil rigs, and on
isolated rocks in strong tidal currents. On a
very low spring tide it is possible to find some
of these deeper-water anemones by searching
in gulleys and kelp beds normally inaccessible.
Some anemones live on the shells occupied by
hermit crabs – in return for providing some
protection, the anemone picks up scraps left
over from the crab's meals.

Shells of scallops and
oysters dredged up from
below the low-water mark
sometimes have plumose
anemones growing on them,
so try to check the catches of
fishing boats. At very low
spring tides check the
supports of piers and jetties
for plumose anemones.

BURROWING ANEMONE ▷
Sagartia troglodytes
H 4cm. Suckers on column.
Two colour varieties in
different habitats.

PARASITIC ANEMONE ▽
Calliactis parasitica
L 8cm. Column long,
tentacles numerous;
attached to hermit-crab
shells.

PLUMOSE ANEMONE ▽
Metridium senile
H 10cm. Tentacles fine and
numerous; several colour
varieties.

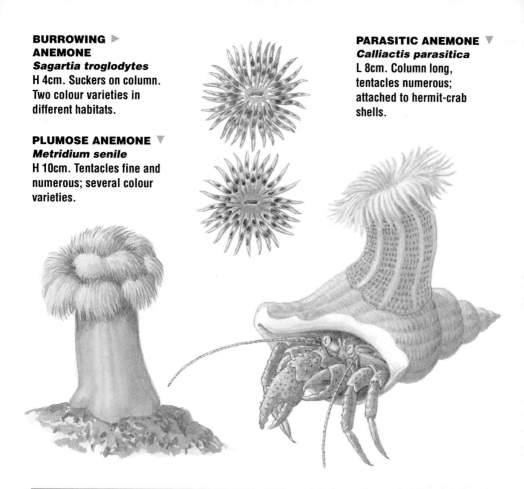

HOW TO WATCH

The dahlia anemone can be difficult to spot, despite its large size, because it camouflages itself by sticking pieces of gravel and shell to its warty column. This, coupled with its habit of living in shady places, means it can easily be overlooked. A tiny spider crab is often found living inside the ring of tentacles and seems to be quite unharmed by them. Watch a dahlia anemone; and if the crab is present, see what it does if the anemone catches something.

MARINE WORMS

RAGWORM
Hediste (Nereis)
diversicolor
L 12cm. Four eyes and four
pairs of tentacles on head;
very colourful, with red line
along dorsal surface.

GENERAL FEATURES

Marine worms are found in a wide variety of
habitats and on all levels of the shore. Most
have segmented bodies, but ribbon worms are
unsegmented and have very long slimy bodies.
The segmented worms have bristles on their
bodies, which are often used to aid movement.
Most marine worms are camouflaged and
difficult to find, but some have bright colours
and therefore look very striking when out of
their usual habitat.

HABITS

Marine worms can be carnivores, herbivores
or scavengers and may be highly active
free-swimming creatures or very secretive,
living in tiny crevices or deep in mud.

The bristles on the side of
the ragworm form tiny
paddles. By flexing its body
and beating the flattened
bristles it is able to move
easily in open water,
although it spends much of
its time buried.

SEA MOUSE ▽
Aphrodite aculeata
L 20cm. Underside flat, back domed. Green and grey iridescent hair.

RED RIBBON WORM ▷
Lineus ruber
L 20cm. Smooth unsegmented body, three or four eyes either side of head.

KING RAGWORM ▷
Neanthes (Nereis) virens
L 40cm. Thick body, many paddle-like lobes. Green with purple tinge.

Polydora ciliata ▽
L 3cm. Bores into oyster shells and limestone.

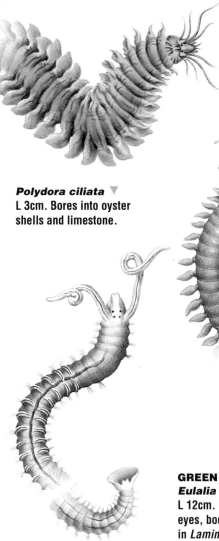

PADDLE WORM △
Phyllodoce paretti
L 30cm. Two eyes and four antennae on head. Very colourful, lives under stones.

GREEN LEAF WORM △
Eulalia viridis
L 12cm. One pair of black eyes, body dark green; lives in *Laminaria* holdfasts.

TUBE-BUILDING WORMS

GENERAL FEATURES

Some marine worms live in tubes, which they build out of sand grains. The tubes may be so numerous that they form huge reefs. Others form sandy tubes which are flexible and move with the current as they stick out of the sea bed. Tubes can also be made out of a chalky substance secreted by the worm.

HABITATS

Some worms live on shells or seaweeds without harming them; they simply attach their tubes to them. The empty tubes are common objects on the strand line and are easily found if shells of large molluscs or the holdfasts of kelps are examined. Some live on rocks and pebbles from the middle shore to beyond the low-tide mark.

Tube-building

The honeycomb worm, *Sabellaria alveolata* (below), uses large, coarse sand grains to build its tubes and forms large colonies resembling honeycombs. These are fixed to rocks, but sometimes the colonies grow so large that the rocks are hidden. Exposed shores where there are rock outcrops and areas of sand are ideal, as the wave action sweeps a constant supply of building material over the worm's colony.

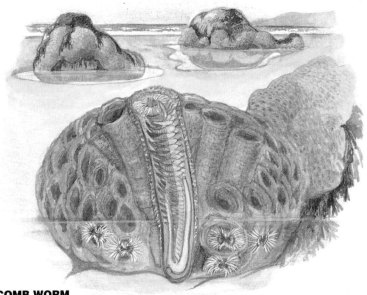

HONEYCOMB WORM
Sabellaria alveolata
L 4cm. Makes sand-grain
tubes in large colonies.

◄ *Spirorbis borealis*
L 0.35 cm. Makes tiny coiled tube on serrated wrack, etc, on middle shore.

TUBE WORM ▽
Hydroides norvegica
L 3cm. Makes cylindrical twisted tube. Head is thistle-like.

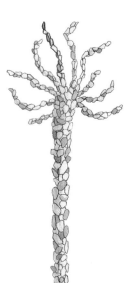

TUBE WORM ▲
Filograna implexa
Forms tangle of minute white tubes on pebbles and shells. Mouth may be bell-shaped.

KEEL WORM ▲
Pomatoceros triqueter
L 2.5cm. Makes triangular, keeled tube on stones, tapering towards tail.

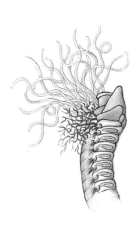

SAND MASON ▲
Lanice conchilega
L 30cm. Long tube of sand grains, with ragged end protruding from sand.

PEACOCK WORM ▲
Sabella pavonia
L 25cm. Long flexible tube; colourful gills form crown.

BURROWING WORMS

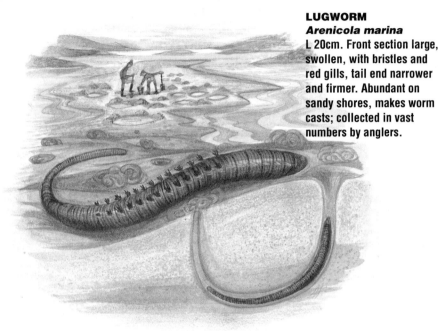

LUGWORM
Arenicola marina
L 20cm. Front section large, swollen, with bristles and red gills, tail end narrower and firmer. Abundant on sandy shores, makes worm casts; collected in vast numbers by anglers.

GENERAL FEATURES

There is a rich supply of food available in sand and mud on sheltered shores and many species of worm make use of this, but they themselves may become food for other creatures so they remain hidden most of the time. They usually have feathery gills projecting from their bodies to take up oxygen; and tentacles which can sweep over the mud for food particles, or a flexible mouth which can take in sand or mud.

HABITS

Sheltered muddy shores, such as in quiet backwaters of estuaries, are home for many worms. They are normally unable to make permanent burrows, but make a temporary tube and seek shelter beneath stones or shells, extending their feeding tentacles over the mud. Lugworms are able to make burrows in sand and line them with mucus.

Lugworms are easily located by their casts, and can be dug up intact with care. They may be 35cm deep in the sand. If a lugworm is examined in water, the gills will be clearly seen, and if it is handled gently the strong bristles will be detected. A lugworm placed on the sand surface will very quickly bury itself again.

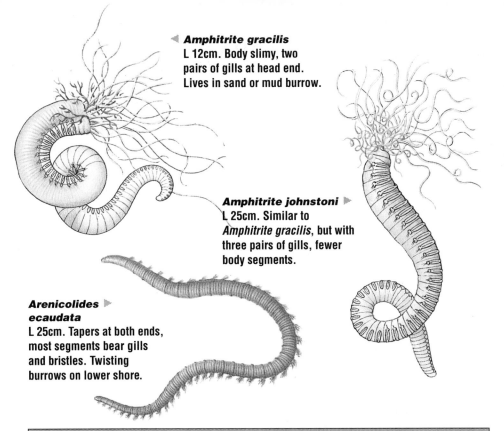

Amphitrite gracilis
L 12cm. Body slimy, two pairs of gills at head end. Lives in sand or mud burrow.

Amphitrite johnstoni
L 25cm. Similar to *Amphitrite gracilis*, but with three pairs of gills, fewer body segments.

Arenicolides ecaudata
L 25cm. Tapers at both ends, most segments bear gills and bristles. Twisting burrows on lower shore.

PROJECT

The bright red gills of *Amphitrite johnstoni* (right) enable it to take up oxygen from water while its body is buried in mud which may have little oxygen. The worm remains concealed, often beneath a stone. Watch how only the tentacles emerge to sweep for food.

The sand mason (left) builds flexible tubes of quite large sand grains, with one, ragged, end protruding into the water. At low tide, look for the tubes which lay flat on the sand, and how, when the tide is in, they float upwards and the fan-like feeding tubes emerge. Always take care not to be caught by incoming tides.

77

MOLLUSCS – LIMPETS

GENERAL FEATURES

Molluscs are soft-bodied and without segments. Their bodies are usually protected by thick shells and they all possess an important muscular organ known as the foot. In the chitons, snails and sea slugs it is adapted for creeping movement or for holding on to rocks, and in the bivalves it is used for burrowing in sand or mud. The shells of molluscs are highly individual structures with many beautiful shapes and colours.

If limpet shells are marked with nail varnish in such a way that the mark lines up with a mark on the rock, it is possible to check if they return to exactly the same position after feeding trips.

HABITATS

Molluscs live at all levels on the shore and in a great range of habitats. They are extremely abundant in some areas. Their empty shells often form huge deposits on the strand line.

COMMON LIMPET
Patella vulgata
L 8cm. Oval outline and conical shape with strong ribbing, and often with barnacles and green algae growing on it. Foot dirty green, inside of shell yellowish.

COAT-OF-MAIL SHELL
Lepidochitona cinereus
L 3cm. Shell keeled and made of eight overlapping plates.

TORTOISESHELL LIMPET ▷
Acmaea tessulata
L 2.5cm. Shallow cone shape, smooth surface, tortoiseshell markings.

◁ **WHITE TORTOISESHELL LIMPET**
Tectura virginica
(Acmaea virginea)
L 1.25cm. Flat cone, smooth surface, pinkish-white markings.

BLUE-RAYED LIMPET ▷
Helcion pellucida
L 2cm. Smooth, oval-shaped, orange or dark brown, with rays of iridescent blue dots.

CHINA LIMPET ◁
Patella ulyssiponensis
L 7cm. Pear-shaped flattened shell, foot orange; shell like porcelain inside.

KEYHOLE LIMPET ▷
Diodora apertura
L 4cm. Conical shell, fine ribbing, hole at apex.

Limpets are common molluscs on most rocky shores and feed on microscopic algae which cover exposed rock surfaces. They move slowly over the rocks, scraping algae off with their rough tongues. They are able to live in very exposed places.

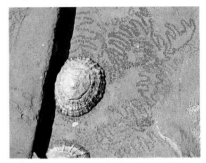

The limpet's foot is very strong and grips the rock tightly. In order to make a good seal the shell grows to fit the contours of the rock, and the limpet clamps itself down in precisely the same position each time it returns to its own piece of rock after a feeding trip. The feeding trails left by limpets look like tiny zig-zag lines on rock surfaces. They can usually be traced back to a feeding limpet. Check the lines to see if they overlap or keep within small areas. Territorial behaviour would mean that each limpet kept to its own feeding area and did not enter another's territory.

SLIT LIMPET △
Emarginula reticulata
L 2cm. Conical, slightly hooked apex, fine ribs, notch at front.

TOPSHELLS AND PERIWINKLES

HABITATS

Large numbers of periwinkles and topshells inhabit sheltered rocky shores, and they are also found in sheltered spots on more exposed shores and in estuaries. Although widely distributed, individual species have their own preferences for different zones and habitats. It will be possible to list them according to the zone of the shore they are found on.

HABITS

Topshells and periwinkles are grazers, feeding on microscopic algae and the young stages of larger seaweeds. Many of them are more active at night, and their feeding trails can be seen on the rocks the next day.

Mimics
Flat periwinkles (below) mimic the bladders on bladder wrack in both size and shape, but they are very variable in colour. Bright colours predominate, but it is usually possible to find many shades from almost white to very dark brownish-black, although orange-yellow is very common. The colours may be a further form of camouflage, because the colours of the seaweed bladders vary at times.

FLAT PERIWINKLE
Littorina obtusata
H 1.5cm. Flattened blunt spiral with large aperture. Shell thick and smooth, but with very fine grooves. Many colour forms.

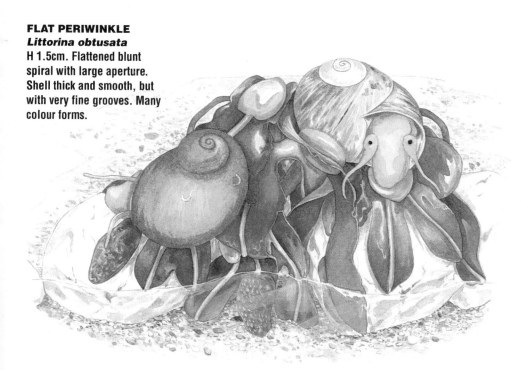

SMALL PERIWINKLE ▽
Littorina neritoides
H 0.7cm. Shell pointed and smooth, very fragile.

ROUGH PERIWINKLE ▽
Littorina saxatilis
H 1.5cm. Pointed, with ridged surface; colours variable.

BANDED CHINK SHELL
Lacuna vincta
H 1cm. Conical and pointed, looks thin and glossy.

◁ EDIBLE PERIWINKLE
Littorina littorea
H 3cm. Thick, pointed, with fine ridges. Mostly dark with stripes. Very common.

◁ PAINTED TOPSHELL
Calliostoma zizyphinum
H 2.5cm. Tall pointed cone, flattened base, glossy.

PURPLE TOPSHELL ▷
Gibbula umbilicalis
D 1.5cm. Shell flattened, brownish-green with purple rays.

◁ GREY TOPSHELL
Gibbula cineraria
H 1.5cm. A slightly flattened cone, pinkish-grey with fine, darker stripes.

PROJECT

Periwinkles and topshells are very active at night and can be seen moving slowly over rocks and in pools with the foot extended and a pair of tentacles visible at the front. By using a torch their feeding tracks should be clearly visible; they can sometimes be traced back to a crevice, where many hide.

TOOTHED OR THICK TOPSHELL
Monodonta lineata
H 2.5cm. Conical, solid, with mother-of-pearl lining.

WHELKS AND OTHER PREDATORS

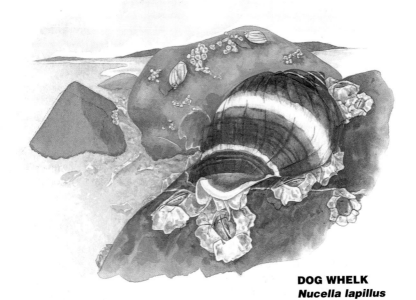

DOG WHELK
Nucella lapillus
H 4cm. Shell solid, pointed, with groove in aperture and sometimes several teeth on rim. Usually white, but variable and may be banded.

GENERAL FEATURES

Bivalves are found washed ashore with circular holes drilled through the shell near the hinge – the result of an attack by a predator.

HABITS

Some molluscs have become highly efficient predators, attacking other molluscs or, in some cases, barnacles or colonial sea squirts. Some scavenge and are able to detect dead fish or other food at a great distance. The tongue is often modified to form a drill-like structure which penetrates the shell of the prey. It is often assisted by a strong acid which dissolves the shell. When a hole has been made, digestive juices are squirted into the shell and the victim is killed and digested before being sucked out of its shell.

Whelks and oyster drills have a groove through one side of the opening. Put a live whelk or oyster drill in some seawater and watch it move. Look carefully to see what emerges from the shell's groove.

ARCTIC COWRIE ▽
Trivia arctica
L 1.2cm. Similar to European cowrie but no spots.

THICK-LIPPED ▲ DOG WHELK
Nassarius incrassatus
H 1.5cm. Ridged and lined; aperture has thick lip.

OYSTER DRILL OR ▲ STING WINKLE
Ocenebra erinacea
H 5cm. Shell solid and roughly ridged. Groove in aperture closed to form a tube.

◀ EUROPEAN COWRIE
Trivia monacha
L 1.2cm. Oval with slit-like opening. Pink-brown with three spots.

COMMON WHELK ▽
Buccinum undatum
H 8cm. Pointed, ribs, fine lines. Large aperture with smooth edge.

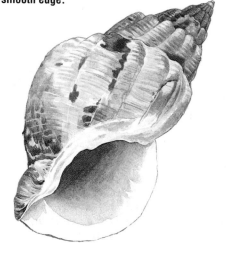

PROJECT

Dog whelks are usually white (below), but banded forms also occur (bottom). One theory to explain the banding is that if whelks prey alternately on barnacles and then mussels they take in light and then dark pigments, producing dark and light colours in their own shells. Look for whelks in areas where there are no mussels to see if banded forms occur there.

PREDATORS AND SCAVENGERS

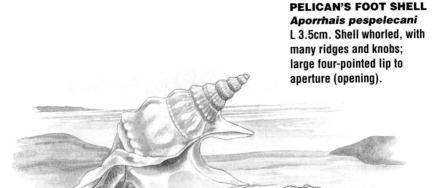

PELICAN'S FOOT SHELL
Aporrhais pespelecani
L 3.5cm. Shell whorled, with
many ridges and knobs;
large four-pointed lip to
aperture (opening).

HABITS

A number of predators have a highly developed
foot which enables them to move swiftly
through sand and mud. They are able to locate
burrowing bivalves and trap them with the foot
while they drill through the shell with their
tongue. Many stranded bivalve shells will show
the results of predation by necklace shells,
bearing smooth round holes with a slightly
bevelled edge.

GENERAL FEATURES

Necklace shells are so called because they lay
their eggs in ribbons of sand and mucus; the
eggs look like a neck-band, or sometimes like
the rim of a piece of pottery. They are very
common below the low-water mark on sandy
shores, and prey on the abundant bivalves
which live there.

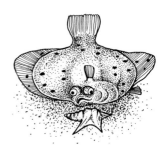

The pelican's foot shell has a
large outer lip which bears
three or four points. As the
mollusc develops, the lip
grows larger and larger. This
may act as a deterrent to
predators like flatfish, which
find the shell awkward in
their small mouths.

NETTED DOG WHELK ▽
Hinia (Nassarius)
reticulatus
H 3.5cm. Many ribs, aperture
has toothed outer lip.

COMMON WENTLETRAP ▽
Clathrus clathrus
H 4cm. Elongated, many
sculptured ridges. Usually
white, but colour varies.

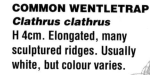

△
COMMON NECKLACE SHELL
Lunatia poliana (Natica alderi)
H 1.5cm. Shell rounded, with large
aperture. Buff-coloured with
reddish streaks.

◁ **BONNET LIMPET OR**
HUNGARIAN CAP
Capulus ungaricus
D 5cm. Bonnet-shaped,
slightly hooked apex.

NEEDLE SHELL △
Bittium reticulatum
H 1.5cm. Narrow, with small
aperture. Finely sculptured
surface.

HOW TO WATCH

Living necklace (right) and pelican's
foot shells are hard to find, but
may be caught by using a shrimp
net in shallow water at low tide.
If the net is pushed firmly through
the sand so that it catches
whatever is living just below the
surface, they may be trapped,
along with the commoner bivalves
which also live there. On the first
high tide after a strong gale the
shells will be found on the strand
line, but they will not live long out
of water, and they will soon be
eaten by gulls. The empty shells
are very common on the strand
line of exposed sandy beaches.

SAND-DWELLING GASTROPODS

GENERAL FEATURES

Sea slugs are molluscs in which the shell is absent, or reduced to a very small structure. The unsegmented body and muscular foot are present, but the body is often adorned by beautifully coloured feathery gills. Some sea slugs have excellent camouflage, but others are brightly coloured and warn predators off with their conspicuous markings. Many feed on sponges, sea mats or sea squirts, but some feed on algae. The banded actaeon has a thick bullet-like shell completely hidden by the body, so is not typical of the other sea slugs.

HABITATS

Sea slugs are mostly confined to shallow water, or deep rock pools from the middle shore downwards. Several species visit the shore to lay their eggs, in long sinuous ribbons.

Sea hare

The sea hare (below) is a large sea slug with a delicate shell, almost enclosed by the body. It is a dark red-brown colour when young, becoming green-brown when older. Its colourings help it to hide amongst seaweeds on the lower shore, and especially amongst eelgrass in the lower reaches of estuaries. Its unusual defence mechanism can best be seen by putting a specimen in a container of seawater, when it will after a short time release a beautiful purple dye into the water.

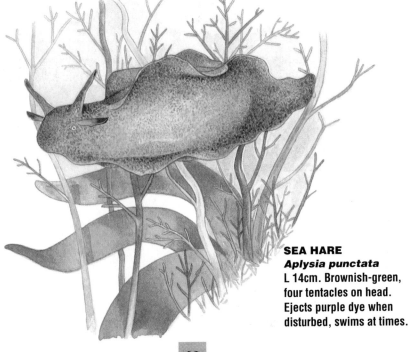

SEA HARE
Aplysia punctata
L 14cm. Brownish-green, four tentacles on head. Ejects purple dye when disturbed, swims at times.

SEA LEMON ▷
Archidoris pseudoargus
L 7cm. Body warty, two
tentacles and ring of
branching gills. Yellowish
with brown markings.

SLIPPER LIMPET ▽
Crepidula fornicata
L 4cm. Oval with very large
aperture, slightly coiled
apex.

GREEN SEA SLUG ▽
Elysia viridis
L 3cm. No shell or gills.
Lobes on side of body. Green
with whiter spots. Lives on
green seaweeds.

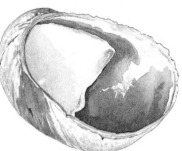

BANDED ACTAEON ▲
Actaeon tornatilis
L 2cm. Pink-brown with
white banding.

LAVER SPIRE SHELL ▽
Hydrobia ulvae
H 0.6cm. Small, coiled, with
blunt apex. Brown to yellow.
Common in muddy estuaries.

◁ **TURRET OR TOWER SHELL**
Turritella communis
L 6cm. Very narrow, sharply
pointed. Finely sculptured
spiral ridges.

HOW TO WATCH

Tufted red and green seaweeds on
the middle and lower shore are
good sites for sea slugs. Collect
weed samples and place them in a
dish of seawater. After a short time
the sea slugs will crawl out. Look
on lower-shore rocks in spring for
eggs of the sea lemon and search
around colonies of breadcrumb
sponge and sea mats for feeding
sea slugs (right). Actaeons can be
caught by dredging off sandy
beaches at low tide; empty shells
are common on strand lines.

COCKLES AND OTHER BIVALVES

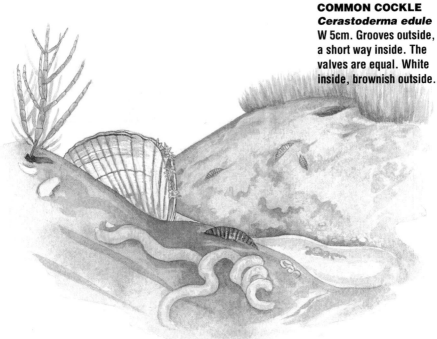

GENERAL FEATURES

Bivalves are molluscs which have a shell in two hinged, usually equal-sized, parts. The foot is often an organ for burrowing, and can sometimes be used for rapid movements. Bivalves are filter feeders, drawing in a current of water and extracting food particles from it. A few bivalves are able to swim by a type of jet-action; the valves are snapped together and the mollusc moves backwards. The shape of the shell, the arrangement of teeth in the valve and the habitat are important features when identifying molluscs.

HABITATS

Many bivalves burrow into sand or mud, but some attach themselves to rocks by sticky threads. Some can burrow into rocks, using a drilling motion and sharp ridges on the shell.

Living cockles can be found on exposed mud or sand at low tide, with half of the shell protruding. Tap a shell gently and a jet of water will squirt out if it is alive. Remove one from the sand and place it on its side in a shallow pool to watch the burrowing action of the foot.

GREAT SCALLOP ⬆
Pecten maximus
W 15cm. Upper valve flat,
with rounded ribs. Lower
valve concave.

Arctica islandica ▽
W 12.5cm. Very heavy, with
black outer 'skin'; valves
equal.

DOG COCKLE ▽
Glycymeris glycymeris
W 6.5cm. Valves equal, 12
teeth each hinge. Crinkled
edges, patterned outside.

HEART SHELL ⬆
Glossus humanus
W 10cm. Curves away from
hinge, heart-shaped end
view. Solid, heavy, with black
outer 'skin'.

COMMON NUT SHELL ⬆
Nucula nucleus
W 1.25cm. Crinkled edges,
brown outer 'skin'.

SPINY COCKLE OR ⬆
RED NOSE
Acanthocardia aculeata
W 10cm. Valves equal,
toothed edges, ribs have
spines.

VARIEGATED SCALLOP ⬆
Chlamys varia
L 6cm. Valves slightly
different, one 'wing' only.

SAND-DWELLING BIVALVES

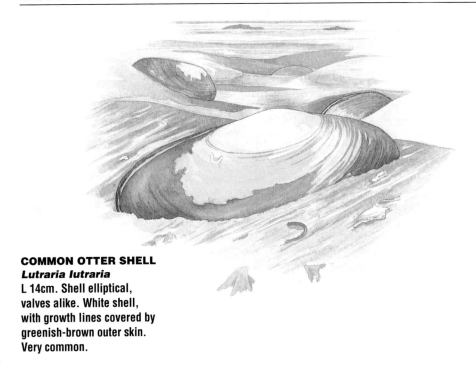

COMMON OTTER SHELL
Lutraria lutraria
L 14cm. Shell elliptical,
valves alike. White shell,
with growth lines covered by
greenish-brown outer skin.
Very common.

GENERAL FEATURES

Bivalves which live buried in sand usually have
streamlined shells which help them burrow
rapidly into the sand if danger threatens.
The foot can be pushed into the sand and then
expanded with body fluids to give a grip.
Strong muscles pull the shell down towards the
foot. Razor shells are extremely efficient at
this movement.

HABITATS

Most sand bivalves live just below the surface,
usually near or below the low-water mark, and
draw in a current of seawater from which they
filter food particles. Many of them have long
siphons which extend up to the surface to
draw in water.

**Sand bivalves often live at
very high densities, with
counts of several hundred of
the same species occurring
in one square metre of
suitable sand. As they all live
at different depths it is
possible to have several
different species in one area.**

GROOVED RAZOR SHELL
Solen marginatus
L 12.5cm. Parallel-sided with equal valves. Groove near front edges of valves.

THIN TELLIN
Tellina tenuis
W 2cm. Delicate, flattened shell, pinkish-orange.

BANDED WEDGE SHELL ▷
Donax vittatus
W 3.75cm. Valves alike, toothed edge. Colourful, often purple or orange.

THICK TROUGH SHELL
Spisula solida
W 4.5cm. Solid, finely ridged, dirty white.

POD RAZOR SHELL
Ensis siliqua
L 20cm. Parallel-sided, valves open at either end, glossy and finely-lined.

RAYED TROUGH SHELL ▷
Mactra corallina
W 5cm. Triangular, valves equal. Shiny and pale purple-white inside.

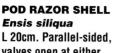

PULLET CARPET SHELL
Venerupis pullastra
W 5cm. Shell oval, dirty white.

WARTY VENUS ▽
Venus verrucosa
L 6.25cm. Heavy, with strong ridges outside, toothed edge.

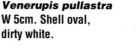

STRIPED VENUS
Venus striatula
W 4.5cm. Triangular with rounded corners, ridged outside with brown rays.

MUD-DWELLERS AND SHIPWORM

GENERAL FEATURES

Mud is a very fertile habitat, but there is very little oxygen below the surface. Therefore, mud-dwellers usually extend long tubes up to the surface; in this way the body of the mollusc remains hidden, but it is able to feed and breathe easily from the water above. Each tide brings a fresh supply of food and oxygen, so there is no need for the molluscs to move.

HABITS

The siphons are sometimes long and worm-like, sweeping over the mud in search of food particles, whilst others are more solid and inflexible. The sand gaper is unable to burrow back into its feeding position if it is removed from the mud, so any specimens collected for study should be returned safely.

Shipworms are molluscs with reduced shells which burrow into and digest wood in ships, piers and driftwood. The shell is tiny but the tube is lined with chalk. The body looks like a long pink worm.

PEPPERY FURROW SHELL
Scrobicularia plana
W 6cm. Shell flattened and delicate. Valves similar, dirty white outside. Siphons long and worm-like. Abundant on muddy shores in estuaries.

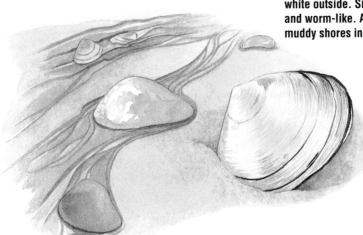

Mud-dwelling molluscs can be collected by digging carefully into mud from the middle shore down. Using a coarse-mesh garden sieve, filter the mud to trap the molluscs. The peppery furrow shell (illustrated) and baltic tellin are quite frequently found in this way. If some are placed on the surface, preferably in a shallow pool, their burrowing action can be observed. Specimens put in a shaded container of seawater will extend their siphons if not disturbed.

BLUNT GAPER ▽
Mya truncata
L 6.5cm. Solid, very blunt-ended and open. Massive siphon.

SAND GAPER △
Mya arenaria
L 15cm. Oblong outline with one valve deeper than the other. Long siphon.

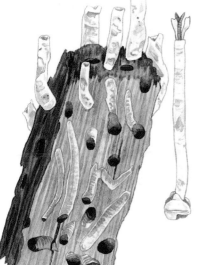

SHIPWORM
Teredo navalis
L 25cm. Shell almost absent. Very destructive to submerged wood.

BALTIC TELLIN ▷
Macoma balthica
W 2.5cm. Oval and plump. Alternate pink and white bands. Very common.

ROCK-DWELLING BIVALVES

COMMON MUSSEL
Mytilus edulis
L 10cm. Triangular; glossy
when small, darker and
encrusted when older.
Forms large colonies.

HABITS

Some filter-feeding bivalves have lost the ability
to move freely. Instead they fix themselves to
rocks. Mussels are well adapted to exposed
situations as their shells are strong. They are
fixed by strong, flexible byssus threads which
are glued to the rock. These hold the mussel
firmly in place, yet allow a certain degree of
movement. The shells gape open very slightly,
exposing the short siphons.

GENERAL FEATURES

Mussels draw in large quantities of seawater,
filtering out plankton. Unfortunately they also
filter out pollutants and harmful micro-
organisms, and can be responsible for shellfish
poisoning. They are very common near outfalls
and inlet pipes to power stations, blocking pipes
when they form huge colonies.

Look for mussels on exposed
rocks, and around the base of
piers and jetties. In winter,
watch eider ducks diving;
mussels are their main food.
Tug at a fixed mussel shell to
test the byssus threads, and
look at the way they are
glued to the rock.

The common piddock is able to bore its way into solid limestone rock by grinding its shell against the rock. As it bores in, the hole becomes larger to accommodate the growing mollusc, but the entrance hole remains roughly the same size; the piddock is therefore trapped. It feeds by drawing in seawater through its siphon. Look at the base of limestone and sandstone cliffs for piddock holes. Visit a piddock colony at night and tap on the rocks with a hammer to watch the piddocks glow in the dark.

▲ **COMMON SADDLE OYSTER**
Anomia ephippium
W 6cm. Lower valve crescent-shaped, upper flat; shell grows to fit shape of rocks.

▲ **HORSE MUSSEL**
Modiolus modiolus
L 15cm. Thick and swollen, valves similar; purplish-brown, may have algae on.

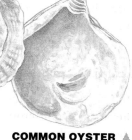

COMMON PIDDOCK ▼
Pholas dactylus
L 13cm. Long; delicate, sharp rays. Unable to close fully. White inside and out.

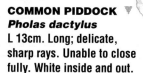

COMMON OYSTER ▲
Ostrea edulis
W 7.5cm. Irregular edge. Often with holes made by boring sponge. At low water level and below.

CEPHALOPODS

COMMON CUTTLEFISH
Sepia officinalis
L 30cm. Broad, flattened
body, fins on both sides.
Colour very variable, usually
striped with brown.

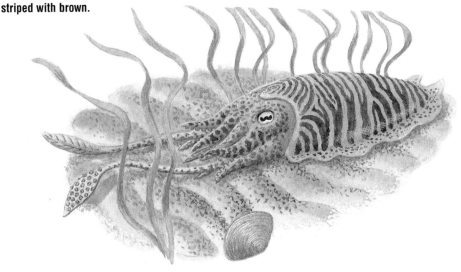

GENERAL FEATURES

Cephalopods are molluscs which have no external shell. The foot has become modified and usually consists of tentacles with powerful suckers. The body can be propelled by water squirted out of a siphon, and in the case of the cuttlefish a membrane along the side of the body ripples in a wave-like motion to aid swimming. The mouth has powerful beak-like jaws.

HABITS

Body colour can be changed rapidly, and seems to vary according to the moods and surroundings of the individual. As a defence mechanism, a cloud of dark, inky dye can be squirted at attackers. In British waters most cephalopods are small and easily overlooked.

The internal shell of the cuttlefish, known as the cuttlebone, is a common object on the strand line. Check for signs of damage by predators. Fossil remains of cuttlebones can be found in limestone on some beaches. The squid has a narrow pen-like shell which is often overlooked.

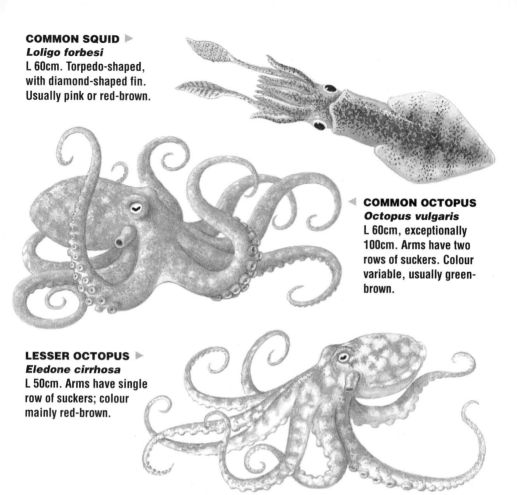

COMMON SQUID ▷
Loligo forbesi
L 60cm. Torpedo-shaped,
with diamond-shaped fin.
Usually pink or red-brown.

◁ **COMMON OCTOPUS**
Octopus vulgaris
L 60cm, exceptionally
100cm. Arms have two
rows of suckers. Colour
variable, usually green-
brown.

LESSER OCTOPUS ▷
Eledone cirrhosa
L 50cm. Arms have single
row of suckers; colour
mainly red-brown.

HOW TO WATCH

Cuttlefish eggs look like bunches of
dark grapes and are laid on
eelgrass and other plants in
sheltered places. Before spawning
in the spring, cuttlefish gather in
sheltered creeks in estuaries and
saltmarshes. The eggs can be found
by dredging through submerged
algae and eelgrass at low water.
Take care not to dislodge too many
as they will not develop if they are
floating in the sea.

BARNACLES

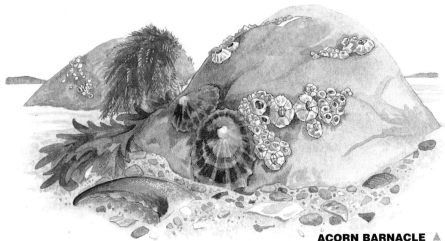

ACORN BARNACLE
Semibalanus balanoides
W 1.3cm. Six ridged plates,
diamond-shaped aperture.

GENERAL FEATURES

Barnacles are closely related to crabs. Like
crabs, they have segmented bodies, but they
are fixed to rocks by the backs of their heads
and surrounded by a shell, and never change
position. Their legs are modified to form feeding
organs; they beat them in the water to draw
food particles into the shell.

HABITS

Barnacles produce millions of larvae like water
fleas. When they detect a chemical left on rocks
by old barnacles, they settle in those spots, and
grow their shell. Stalked barnacles attach
themselves to floating objects, feeding in the
same way. Some barnacles are parasites inside
the bodies of crabs.

STAR BARNACLE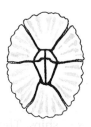
Chthamalus stellatus
W 1cm. Four side plates
overlap two end plates,
aperture kite-shaped.

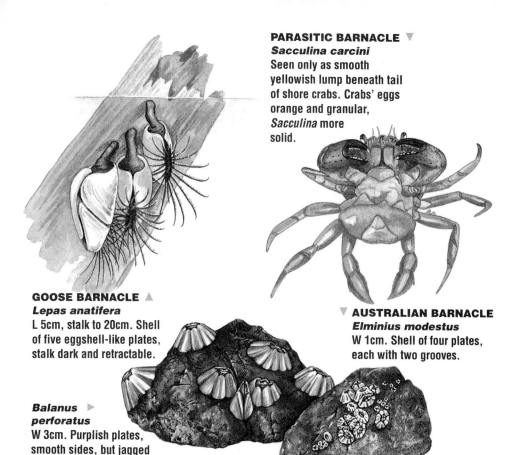

PARASITIC BARNACLE ▽
Sacculina carcini
Seen only as smooth
yellowish lump beneath tail
of shore crabs. Crabs' eggs
orange and granular,
Sacculina more
solid.

GOOSE BARNACLE △
Lepas anatifera
L 5cm, stalk to 20cm. Shell
of five eggshell-like plates,
stalk dark and retractable.

▽ **AUSTRALIAN BARNACLE**
Elminius modestus
W 1cm. Shell of four plates,
each with two grooves.

Balanus ▷
perforatus
W 3cm. Purplish plates,
smooth sides, but jagged
edge and off-centre opening.

HOW TO WATCH

Barnacles can be found on all
levels and on most types of
seashore; they are most common
on very exposed shores where little
else can grow, and they are least
common on very muddy or
polluted shores. They prefer solid
rocks. They also live on crab and
mollusc shells (right) and coat the
hulls of ships. The parasitic barnacle
is found in shore crabs; look for a
crab which has a shell encrusted
by other barnacles and check the
underside for the parasite.

SLATERS AND SANDHOPPERS

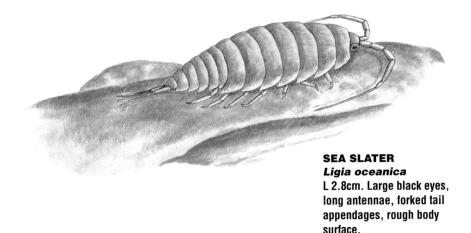

SEA SLATER
Ligia oceanica
L 2.8cm. Large black eyes,
long antennae, forked tail
appendages, rough body
surface.

GENERAL FEATURES

Sea slaters look like giant woodlice and are
closely related to them. They are highly active
creatures, especially at night when they
browse on algae.

HABITATS

Species all have different preferences for zones
and habitats. The common sea slater lives near
the high-tide line and cannot tolerate long
exposure to seawater. Sandhoppers live on the
strand line and scavenge on decaying seaweed
and other debris. The gribble lives in dead
wood and riddles ships' timbers and wooden
piers with tiny holes. Another tiny amphipod,
Chelura terebrans, lives in gribble holes but
cannot bore wood itself.

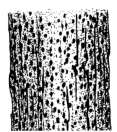

Driftwood often shows signs
of burrowing. Gribbles make
many tiny holes about 3mm
in diameter. Shipworms
make holes about 6mm in
diameter, which are lined
with chalk and may not be
quite so crowded.

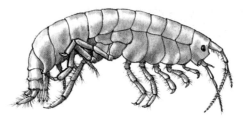

SAND SHRIMP ▲
Gammarus locusta
L 2cm. Body flattened; front
legs for swimming, rear legs
for jumping.

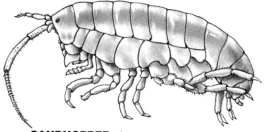

SANDHOPPER ▲
Talitrus saltator
L 2.5cm. Body flattened,
black eyes and black stripe
on back, long antennae.

Idotea baltica ▶
Male 3.5cm, female 1.7cm
long. Oblong body with
keeled back, brown and
slightly mottled.

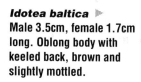

PROJECT

Sea slaters can be difficult to observe
because they hide during the day, so a
visit to the shore at night, preferably
when the tide is falling, will give a
good opportunity to see them feeding.
If you need a torch use it sparingly, as
the slaters will hide if it shines on
them. Look at the uncovered rocks on
the upper shore and the sides of
gulleys, and check washed-up algae on
the strand line.

◀ **GRIBBLE**
Limnoria lignorum
L 0.35cm. Antennae very
short, body oblong, legs
short; burrows into wood.

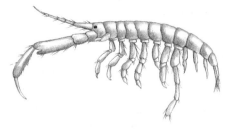

Corophium volutator ▲
L 0.8cm. Lower antennae
very long. Very common in
burrows on muddy shores.

SHRIMPS AND PRAWNS

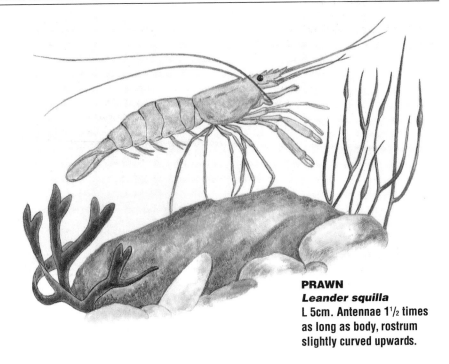

PRAWN
Leander squilla
L 5cm. Antennae 1½ times
as long as body, rostrum
slightly curved upwards.

GENERAL FEATURES

Shrimps and prawns are common crustaceans
on many types of seashore. They are highly
active free-swimming organisms with good
eyesight and long, sensitive antennae. Often the
front one or two pairs of walking legs have tiny
pincers. Between the eyes is a long projection
called the rostrum; this is often a key feature
for identification and should always be checked.

HABITS

Many shrimps and prawns have almost
transparent bodies, and some are able to
change colour to match their surroundings.
The edible shrimp often buries itself in sand,
emerging only at night to feed. Shrimps and
prawns are readily attracted to a bait of dead
fish or mollusc remains.

The shrimps served up in
restaurants look very
different from those caught
on the shore. No shrimp or
prawn looks pink in the sea.
The body pigments are
destroyed by heat and the
pink colour is the result of
being boiled.

CHAMELEON PRAWN ▷
Hippolyte varians
L 2.5cm. Antennae half as
long as body. Colour variable
according to background, but
clear sky-blue at night.

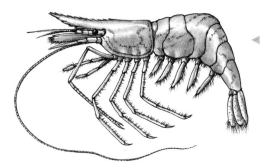

◁ **AESOP PRAWN**
Pandalus montagui
L 4cm. Antennae longer than
body, rostrum curved and
toothed. Common in rock
pools on lower shore.

COMMON SHRIMP ▷
Crangon vulgaris
L 5cm. Antennae shorter than
body, rostrum very small.
Common in estuaries and on
lower shore.

HOW TO WATCH

Sandy pools in estuaries at low
tide are excellent places to look for
shrimps (below). Before disturbing
a pool, look at the sand for signs of
buried shrimps; there may be a
slight ripple in the sand where a
shrimp is hiding. Make a shadow
across the pool to watch the
reactions of hidden shrimps.

A round net is best for catching
prawns (above) in deep pools;
sweep it slowly through the
seaweed. Use a drop net baited
with fish or shellfish to catch
prawns in deep water from a pier.
Remember that **S**hrimps like **S**and,
Prawns like **P**ools.

SPIDER AND MASKED CRAB

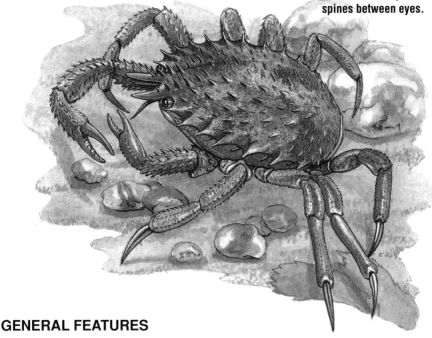

SPINY SPIDER CRAB
Maia squinado
L 18cm. Very spiny, often covered with algae. Two spines between eyes.

GENERAL FEATURES

Crabs are crustaceans with a hard carapace, or shell, two pairs of antennae, stalked eyes and five pairs of walking legs, some armed with pincers. Spider crabs have very long legs and are often extremely agile walkers and climbers. The first pair of legs normally bears pincers. The carapace is often camouflaged with seaweed and may also have sponges and barnacles growing on it. Every time the crab moults, it has to acquire new camouflage.

HABITATS

Spider crabs are common but often overlooked because of their camouflage. Large spider crabs are generally found in deep water, but sometimes become stranded in rock pools.

Using seaweed as a form of camouflage is important to the spider crab, as it enables the crab to get close to its food without being too conspicuous to predators.

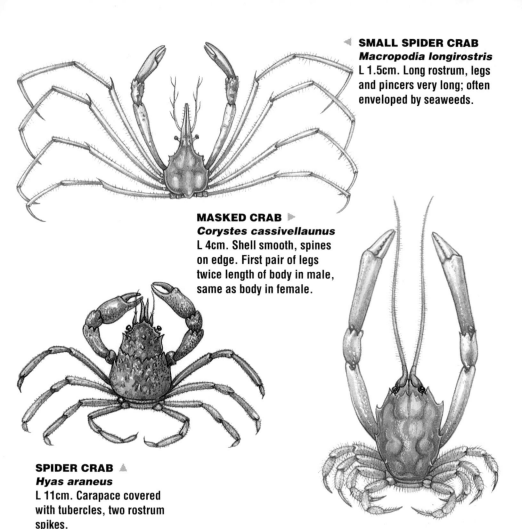

SMALL SPIDER CRAB
Macropodia longirostris
L 1.5cm. Long rostrum, legs and pincers very long; often enveloped by seaweeds.

MASKED CRAB ▷
Corystes cassivellaunus
L 4cm. Shell smooth, spines on edge. First pair of legs twice length of body in male, same as body in female.

SPIDER CRAB ▲
Hyas araneus
L 11cm. Carapace covered with tubercles, two rostrum spikes.

HOW TO WATCH

The masked crab can be difficult to see buried in the sand near the low-water mark. After a storm, many are washed up on the strand line, and live specimens can be seen. At night the crabs emerge from the sand to scavenge on tiny scraps, so a walk along the water's edge at low tide with a shrimp net may be successful. Take care, and don't go alone.

CRABS

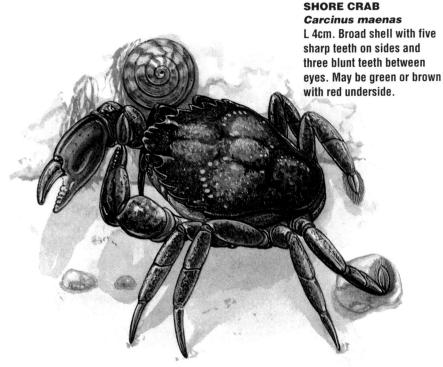

SHORE CRAB
Carcinus maenas
L 4cm. Broad shell with five
sharp teeth on sides and
three blunt teeth between
eyes. May be green or brown
with red underside.

GENERAL FEATURES

The shore crab is one of the commonest
creatures on the seashore, from exposed rocky
shores to muddy estuaries. It has a good set
of pincers, legs adapted for walking and
swimming, and excellent eyesight. The largest
crab is the edible crab, which starts life as a
tiny free-swimming creature like a water-flea,
and then moves to the shore, when it looks like
a miniature adult, gradually growing larger.
As it grows it moves further down the shore.

HABITS

Shore crabs are very lively and are also very
aggressive, readily defending themselves against
predators. Swimming crabs are even more
aggressive, and can also swim very well.

The blue spots on the legs,
and red eyes, of the velvet
swimming crab, are used to
frighten off predators. If the
crab is disturbed, it will
brandish its pincers and
display the bright colours in
a very aggressive way.

EDIBLE CRAB
Cancer pagurus
L 14cm, but specimens on shore usually much smaller. Shell very wide with pie-crust edge. Pincers black-tipped.

HAIRY CRAB ▲
Pilumnus hirtellus
L 1.8cm. Pincers unequal, dark-tipped. Shell hairy, with groove between eyes.

VELVET SWIMMING ▲ CRAB
Liocarcinus puber
L 8cm. 8–10 teeth between red eyes. Carapace hairy.

SWIMMING CRAB ▲
Macropipus depurator
L 4cm. Three sharp teeth between eyes and five teeth on either side. Shell surface rough.

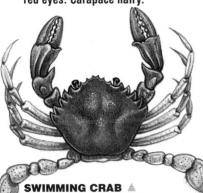

PROJECT

Look for shore crabs beneath stones, under weed and in pools. They will easily be caught in drop nets baited with dead fish. Crabs can be picked up safely by holding the sides of the carapace between finger and thumb. Investigate the undersides of crabs and check on the sex: males have a narrow tail, females have a broader tail.

CRABS

COMMON HERMIT CRAB
Eupagurus bernhardus
L 10cm. Pincers unequal and
have rough surface. Soft
abdomen, red or brown.

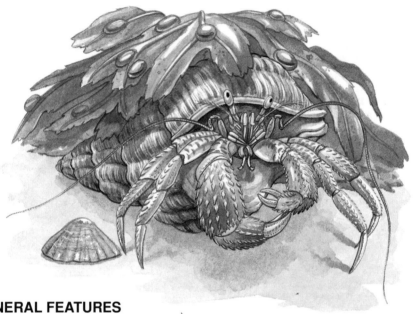

GENERAL FEATURES

Not all crabs have a strong carapace to protect
them. The hermit crab has tough pincers and
walking legs, but its abdomen is completely
unprotected. It uses the abandoned shells of
molluscs as homes, often sharing them with
sponges, anemones and worms.

HABITS

Hermit crabs can withdraw completely into the
shell and guard the entrance with their pincers.
They are highly active scavengers. The pea
crab inhabits a living mollusc shell, such as the
mussel or oyster, entering whilst only a tiny
larva. It feeds on minute particles of food
drawn in by the mollusc. Porcelain crabs hide
under stones or holdfasts.

Some countries have laws
prohibiting the collecting of
shells on the shore in order
to safeguard the hermit crabs
which need them for their
homes. If you are collecting
shells, take great care that
they are not in use by
molluscs or hermit crabs.

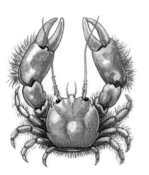

◄ LONG-CLAWED
PORCELAIN CRAB
Psidia longicornis
W 0.6cm. Shell rounded and
shiny, pincers slender. Long
antennae.

BROAD-CLAWED ▲
PORCELAIN CRAB
Porcellana platycheles
L 1.2cm. Shell hairy. Long
antennae. Pincers flattened
with hairy outer edges.

PEA CRAB ▶
Pinnotheres pisum
W 1.5cm, males smaller.
Shell pea-like and smooth.
Lives inside living bivalves.

◄ **CHINESE MITTEN CRAB**
Eriocheir sinensis
L 7cm. Four teeth, pincers
hairy. Shell shiny.

HOW TO WATCH

Look into deep pools for topshells or periwinkles which are more than usually active and aggressive; these will be inhabited by hermit crabs. Turn them over to look for the pincers guarding the aperture. Porcelain crabs (illustrated) can be found by lifting large stones on the lower shore; look on the underside of the stone as well as the rock beneath it, as porcelain crabs often cling on to rock surfaces. Check any kelp holdfasts as these make excellent hiding places.

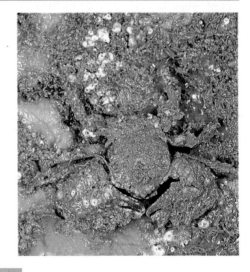

LOBSTERS AND SEA SPIDER

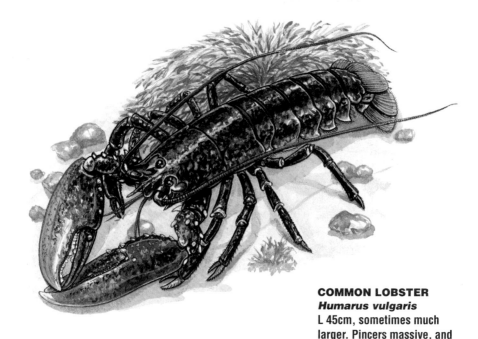

GENERAL FEATURES

The lobster has a thick carapace. Its pincers are
powerful weapons underwater, but out of water
they are so heavy that they cannot be used so
easily. They should still be handled extremely
carefully, however. The spiny lobster, or
crayfish, has no pincers but it is armed with
very sharp spines. Squat lobsters are much
smaller and their abdomen is folded under the
thorax. They are armed with long slender
pincers and can be quite fierce when picked up.

HABITS

The lobster can move easily over the sea bed in
search of its prey. It can detect a dead fish from
a great distance, and this often leads it into
lobster pots baited with fish, from which it is
then unable to get out.

Sea spider
The sea spider (right) is not
a crustacean, but is in a
class of its own called
Pycnogonida. It appears to
have no body at all, as its
abdomen is very slender. The
internal organs grow down
inside the legs, and the head
and thorax are joined
together to form a strange-
looking proboscis with a tiny
mouth at the tip. In addition
to the four pairs of walking
legs, there is a pair which
carries the female's eggs.
It lives on the lower shore
and in shallow water.

Small lobsters can be found on sheltered rocky shores in deep pools or gulleys at the low-water mark, and it is possible to capture them with a strong home-made lobster pot. Use chicken wire rolled into a cylinder for the body and a circular piece of wire for the base. Roll a short cylinder of wire into a cone, and fix it, with the wide end out, to the body of the trap. Place a stone in it to weigh it down, put a piece of dead fish inside it and lower it into a deep pool. Leave it overnight or whilst the tide comes in and goes out again. Don't try unless the weather is very calm.

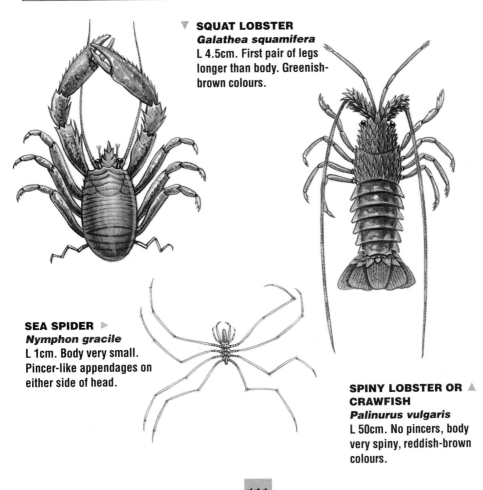

SQUAT LOBSTER
Galathea squamifera
L 4.5cm. First pair of legs longer than body. Greenish-brown colours.

SEA SPIDER ▷
Nymphon gracile
L 1cm. Body very small. Pincer-like appendages on either side of head.

SPINY LOBSTER OR ▲
CRAWFISH
Palinurus vulgaris
L 50cm. No pincers, body very spiny, reddish-brown colours.

STARFISH AND SEA URCHINS

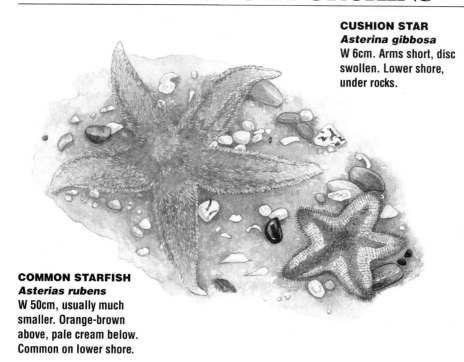

CUSHION STAR
Asterina gibbosa
W 6cm. Arms short, disc
swollen. Lower shore,
under rocks.

COMMON STARFISH
Asterias rubens
W 50cm, usually much
smaller. Orange-brown
above, pale cream below.
Common on lower shore.

GENERAL FEATURES

Starfish have five arms and sea urchins have
five plates fused together to form a shell.
They all have a skeleton of chalky plates, and
spines with tube feet between them. The mouth
is normally on the underside. In sea urchins
the mouth is small and the chalky plates are
arranged to form an intricate structure which
supports the jaw muscles. It is called the
'Aristotle's Lantern' and can usually be found
inside washed-up, empty shells.

HABITS

Starfish have tube feet which are important for
movement and gripping prey. In the sea urchin
they are used mainly for holding on to rocks,
whilst the spines are used for movement.

In many species of starfish
the tube feet are so strong
that they can grip on to the
shell of a bivalve mollusc
like a mussel and slowly pull
it open. The starfish eats the
contents.

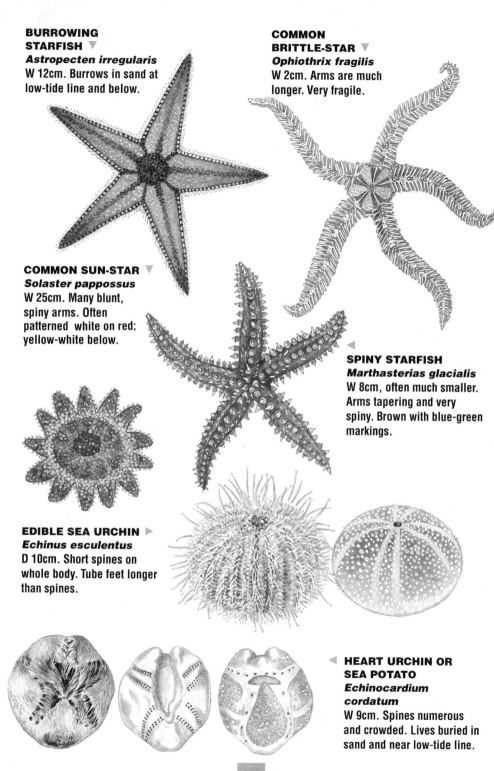

BURROWING STARFISH ▽
Astropecten irregularis
W 12cm. Burrows in sand at low-tide line and below.

COMMON BRITTLE-STAR ▽
Ophiothrix fragilis
W 2cm. Arms are much longer. Very fragile.

COMMON SUN-STAR ▽
Solaster pappossus
W 25cm. Many blunt, spiny arms. Often patterned white on red; yellow-white below.

SPINY STARFISH
Marthasterias glacialis
W 8cm, often much smaller. Arms tapering and very spiny. Brown with blue-green markings.

EDIBLE SEA URCHIN ▷
Echinus esculentus
D 10cm. Short spines on whole body. Tube feet longer than spines.

HEART URCHIN OR SEA POTATO
Echinocardium cordatum
W 9cm. Spines numerous and crowded. Lives buried in sand and near low-tide line.

SEA MATS AND SEA SQUIRTS

GENERAL FEATURES

Sea mats are very small animals living inside tough cases; each is minute, but they form quite large colonies. Each animal has a simple digestive system and a mouth surrounded by a ring of small tentacles. Sea squirts are filter-feeding animals which live inside a tough skin. They have two siphons, and are usually fixed at the base to rocks or seaweeds. Colonial sea squirts, such as the star ascidian, group themselves around a common exhalant siphon.

HABITATS

Some sea-mat colonies form irregular-shaped patches on the surfaces of large seaweeds, whilst others form free-standing tufts or large branched colonies looking like dried seaweed.

Hornwrack
One of the commonest objects on the strand line, especially in the winter, is hornwrack (right). Although it has the appearance of a piece of dried and rough-textured seaweed, it is a large sea mat. It was given the name hornwrack because of its tough horny texture and wrack-like appearance. Like so many animals on the seashore, its appearance is deceiving and it has been given a plant name.

COMMON SEA SQUIRT
Ciona intestinalis
H 12cm. Solitary, with two yellow-rimmed siphons. Semi-transparent with internal organs just visible.

Ascidiella aspera ▷
H 12cm. Oval shaped, with rough textured reddish skin. Common on lower shore.

◁ **HORNWRACK**
Flustra foliacea
H 20cm (colonies). Cells rectangular. Large colonies below low-water mark.

SEA MAT ⬆
Membranipora membranacea
Rectangular cells. Colonies encrust kelp fronds and smooth shells.

STAR ASCIDIAN ⬆
Botryllus schlosseri
Large colonies under stones. Colour may be deep blue, red, yellow or green.

PROJECT

After a winter storm, sea squirts may be found on the strand line. To check if a squirt is still alive, squeeze it very gently; if a jet of water emerges from the lower siphon it is alive. If the squirt is placed in a container of fresh seawater and left to settle for a while it will start to feed. The action of the siphons can be watched by using a pipette to introduce a few drops of water made cloudy with yeast extract near the top siphon.

SHARKS AND RAYS

GENERAL FEATURES

Sharks and rays have a rough skin. The mouth is on the underside of the head and usually armed with powerful teeth. Basking sharks have a huge mouth but no teeth, because they are filter feeders. They swim with their mouths wide open. Skates and rays have flattened bodies, with wing-like projections.

BASKING SHARK ▲
Cetorhinus maximus
L 10–15m. Huge size makes identification easy if close up. Often only fins visible.

HABITS

Some sharks prey on shoaling fishes such as herring and mackerel, whilst others, like the smaller dogfish, are scavengers. Skates and rays remain on the bottom, feeding mostly on small flatfish and crabs.

HOW TO WATCH

In summer basking sharks may come within 2m of rocky shores, especially in hot weather. If the dorsal fin is pointed the shark is young; if it is squarer and flops to one side the shark is an older one.

Skates and rays are much more difficult to see, although their empty black egg cases, or 'mermaids' purses' (left, with empty whelk egg mass and dogfish egg-case), are often found on the strand line. Sometimes after a severe storm a mermaid's purse containing a living embryo is found. This can be observed for some time in a well-aerated aquarium. Both the common skate and thornback ray are frequently caught by fishing boats.

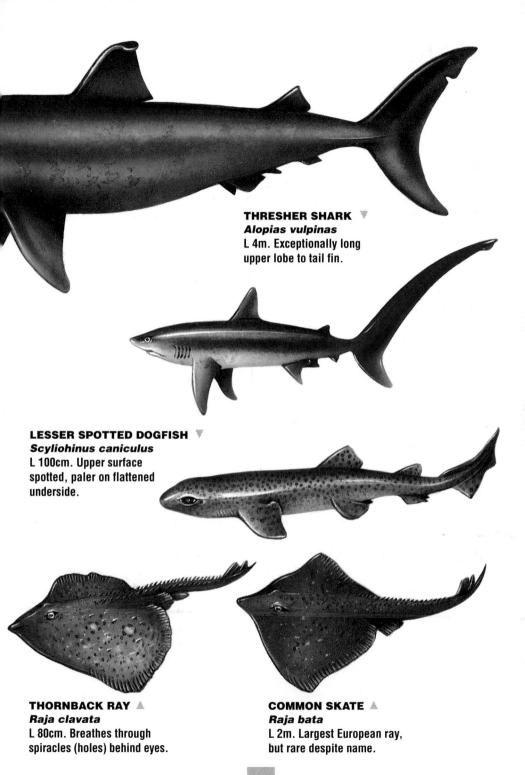

THRESHER SHARK ▽
Alopias vulpinas
L 4m. Exceptionally long
upper lobe to tail fin.

LESSER SPOTTED DOGFISH ▽
Scyliohinus caniculus
L 100cm. Upper surface
spotted, paler on flattened
underside.

THORNBACK RAY △
Raja clavata
L 80cm. Breathes through
spiracles (holes) behind eyes.

COMMON SKATE △
Raja bata
L 2m. Largest European ray,
but rare despite name.

ROCKY-SHORE FISH

GENERAL FEATURES

Some fish are so well adapted to life between the tides that they can even survive for short periods out of water if there is plenty of cover from algae. Many seashore fish are small and perfectly camouflaged, and most of them do not venture into very deep water. Some are the immature stages of fish which live in deeper water as adults.

HABITS

Fish themselves are important predators on the shore, feeding on a variety of smaller organisms. They can usually be caught by netting, although some species are good at hiding in crevices out of reach of predators and nets.

The common blenny, or shanny, is one of the commonest fish on the seashore. It is a lively and inquisitive fish with good eyesight and a large mouth armed with teeth. It is able to catch tiny crabs, crush mollusc and barnacle shells and pursue smaller fish.

COMMON BLENNY
Blennius pholis
L 18cm. Mottled green, but can match surroundings.

FATHER LASHER ▲
Myoxocephalus scorpius
L 30cm. Huge head with sharp spines, fins rounded and mottled.

WORM PIPEFISH ▷
Nerophis lumbriciformis
L 17cm. Body worm-like. Males carry eggs on belly.

15-SPINED STICKLEBACK
Spinachia spinachia
L 15cm. Long snout and stalk-like tail, 15 spines on back.

BLACK GOBY ▲
Gobius niger
L 18cm. Body dark. Male guards eggs laid by female on stones or weed.

TOMPOT BLENNY ▲
Blennius (Parablennius) gattorugine
L 20cm. Tentacle above each eye, banded markings.

BUTTERFISH OR GUNNEL ▲
Pholis gunnellus
L 20cm. Eel-like and slippery. Often under stones on lower shore.

FIVE-BEARDED ROCKLING ▽
Ciliata mustela
L 20cm. Four barbels on snout, one on lower jaw. Mainly brown, paler below.

CORKWING WRASSE ▲
Crenilabrus melops
L 20cm. Very variable but usually greenish males and browner females.

SANDY-SHORE FISH

LESSER WEEVER
Trachinus vipera
L 15cm. Sandy-coloured;
dark dorsal fin. Dorsal fin
can inflict painful sting.

HABITS

Many of the inhabitants of sandy shores have
excellent camouflage and are able to avoid
being spotted by remaining motionless on the
same bed. As a further aid to camouflage they
often flick sand over their bodies with their fins.
Sand gobies bury themselves almost completely,
with only the head and upwards-pointing
mouth exposed.

GENERAL FEATURES

Flatfish have both eyes on the same side of
their heads, and lie in wait on the sea bed for
a passing shrimp or crab. The hooknose often
lives in cloudy water, so it has sensitive bristles
under its mouth to help locate food. Eelgrass
beds are good hiding places for the pipefish.
It twines its tail around the stems.

Place some clean sand in the
bottom of a clear container
and gently pour in some
clear seawater. Allow it to
settle and then place a sand
goby in the container. Watch
its behaviour as it touches
the bottom. Test its reaction
to a shadow moving over
the container.

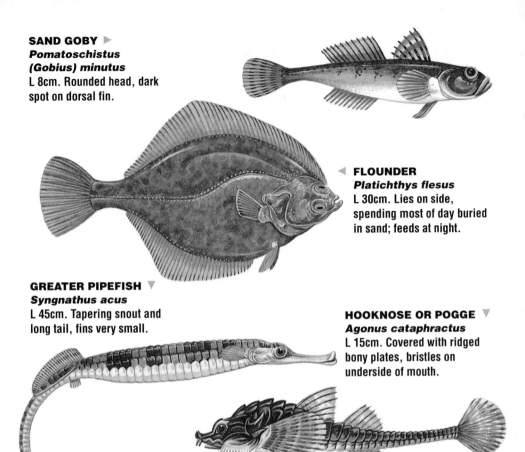

SAND GOBY ▷
*Pomatoschistus
(Gobius) minutus*
L 8cm. Rounded head, dark
spot on dorsal fin.

◁ **FLOUNDER**
Platichthys flesus
L 30cm. Lies on side,
spending most of day buried
in sand; feeds at night.

GREATER PIPEFISH ▽
Syngnathus acus
L 45cm. Tapering snout and
long tail, fins very small.

HOOKNOSE OR POGGE ▽
Agonus cataphractus
L 15cm. Covered with ridged
bony plates, bristles on
underside of mouth.

HOW TO WATCH

Paddling on a sandy beach at low
water will sometimes disturb
bottom-living fish (such as this
flounder), which may be seen
shooting away and settling again
quickly. Tiny flatfish are common
in the upper reaches of estuaries
and can usually be caught in a
shrimp net, but they are very alert
and easily scared so do not allow a
shadow to fall on the water.

SEALS AND OTTER

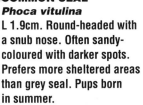

COMMON SEAL
Phoca vitulina
L 1.9cm. Round-headed with
a snub nose. Often sandy-
coloured with darker spots.
Prefers more sheltered areas
than grey seal. Pups born
in summer.

GENERAL FEATURES

Seals need to come to land to breed, and
frequently haul out on rocks to sleep in the
sun. They can spend several weeks far out to
sea, however, and swim and dive extremely
well. They are able to catch large, active fish.

HABITS

Seals are ungainly on land and never move far
from the water; they prefer to be near enough
to jump in at the first sign of danger.
Sometimes seals gather in great numbers, and
their curious moaning calls can be heard from
a distance. Otters are as much at home on the
land as they are in the water and can run and
climb over rocks with ease. They do not
venture as far out to sea as seals, preferring to
hunt much closer to the shore.

The shape of the head of the
two species of seal is
distinctive when seen
clearly. In the grey seal the
nostrils appear almost
vertical, whilst in the
common seal they form
a 'V' shape.

OTTER ▼
Lutra lutra
L 130cm. Long elegant body with tapering tail and blunt muzzle. Dark brown above, white below. Very secretive, mostly nocturnal.

Seals are armed with ▲ powerful teeth and jaws for hunting fish. They have good eyesight, and are also able to catch fish in very cloudy conditions because of their sensitive whiskers.

GREY SEAL ▼
Halichoerus grypus
L 3m. Large head with 'Roman' nose. Mostly grey colouring with darker mottlings. Often on wild rocky shores. Pups born in autumn.

WHALES AND DOLPHINS

PORPOISE
Phocoena phocoena
L 1.8m. Smallest whale, plump with no 'beak'. Back fin small and blunt. Usually in small groups.

GENERAL FEATURES

Whales are true marine mammals. They never come to land except in the case of rare strandings, when they usually die. They breathe air at the surface but can stay underwater for long periods, making very deep dives. The toothed whales catch mainly fish, but the killer whale will also take smaller dolphins. They communicate with each other by means of a variety of sounds, some outside the range of human ears. They often live in large schools, working together to round up shoals of fish.

HABITATS

Pollution, overfishing, abandoned fishing tackle and illegal slaughtering are all taking their toll of whales, which are becoming increasingly rare throughout the world.

Look out to sea for noisy flocks of birds diving for fish; this will be a good place to look for whales, dolphins and porpoises, as they will be attracted to the fish as well.

BOTTLE-NOSED DOLPHIN ▷
Tursiops truncatus
L 4m. Short beak, large
pointed back fin. Commonest
dolphin.

WHITE-SIDED DOLPHIN ▽
Lagenorhynchus acutus
L 2.7m. Short beak. Pale line
on flanks. Sometimes in very
large schools.

LONG-FINNED △
PILOT WHALE
Globicephala melaena
L to 8m. Short beak, bulbous
forehead. Long pointed
flippers. Often in large
schools. Much persecuted.

KILLER WHALE ▽
Orcinus orca
L 9m. Males have long
triangular back fin. White
patches on head and flanks.
Usually in small schools.

INDEX

ILLUSTRATIONS BY

Bernard Thornton Artists: Fred Anderson 18, 24–25; Alma Hathway 46–53, 72–77 Garden Studios: David Ashby 8, 14; Shirley Felts cover · Karen Johnson 9, 116–119, 122–125 · Linden Artists: John Bignall 62–71, 96–97; Gillian Kenny 54–61; Stephen Lings 120–121; Jane Pickering 78–95, 98–99, 112–115; Phil Weare 104–111; David Webb 100–103 · Maltings Partnership 4–7, 10–13, 15–17, 20–23.
Additional black and white line illustrations by Karen Johnson. All other illustrations from Hamlyn's *Guide to Seashores of Britain and Europe*.

The publishers would like to thank the following organisations and individuals for their kind permission to reproduce the photographs in this book:

Biophotos: Heather Angel 43 · Derek Hall 19 top left, 19 centre · Eric and David Hosking: D.P. Wilson 63, 64, 67, 68 · Frank Lane Picture Agency: David T. Grewcock 90; M. Nimmo 6; Peter Reynolds 31; M.J. Thomas 55 · Natural Science Photos: Paul Kaye 50 · Nature Photographers: Front Cover, 25; S.C. Bisserot 83 below, 99, 103 right, 115; N.A. Callow 17; Andrew Cleave 5 above, 7, 9, 19 top right, 33, 35, 41, 49, 66, 70, 76, 79, 81, 83 above, 93, 105, 107, 111; Paul Sterry 21, 47, 57, 59, 65, 69 left, 77 right, 87 above, 101, 103 left, 106, 109, 121; Don Smith 123; J.M. Sutherland 13; Roger Tidman 19 below, 116 · NHPA: A.J. Cambridge 54, 71; Laurie Campbell 39, 77 left; Stephen Dalton 45; Jeff Goodman 69 right; L. Jackman 95; Lacz Lemoine 88; Roger Tidman 124; Roger Waller 25, 87 below.